Christopher Catherwood has taught both European history and church history in the UK and in Virginia, USA, where he is a regular writer in residence for the University of Richmond's History Department. A prolific author, Christopher's published titles include *Five Evangelical Leaders* (1984) and *Why the Nations Rage: Killing in the Name of God* (2002), a study on terrorism and ethnic warfare. He is married and lives in Cambridge, where he teaches at the university on a freelance basis.

Whose Side Is God On?

NATIONALISM AND CHRISTIANITY

Christopher Catherwood

 CHURCH

Church Publishing Incorporated, New York

A catalog record for this book is available from
the Library of Congress

ISBN 0–89869–422–1

Church Publishing Incorporated
445 Fifth Avenue
New York, NY 10016
www.churchpublishing.org

5 4 3 2 1

Printed in Great Britain

To my sister Bethan and brother Jonathan
and
to my brothers-in-law
Sterling and Marshall
and to their splendid little sister
my wife Paulette

Contents

Acknowledgements

Acknowledgements usually end with thanking the long-suffering wife for being so patient while the book was written. I would like to begin with profound thanks to my wife Paulette, without whose encouragement this book would never have been written. She was able to make sure that I had done all the work needed in any given day, and that everything was duly finished. In addition, her talented teaching of so many pupils meant that I was able to concentrate on writing, without having to teach anyone myself during the writing period. I cannot thank her enough! She has also been the perfect critic, without whom I would never get anything worthwhile completed or written.

Editors often get left out, in many cases because they are too modest to want to see their own name in print. So for the successive and immensely patient editors that I had at SPCK, warmest thanks for your patience and for making this into a readable book. In particular I would like to thank Naomi Starkey for commissioning this work, and Alison Barr for waiting long enough to see it finally come to a conclusion.

I am more than grateful as always to the academic homes that I have had during the writing process. I give warmest thanks to Sir Brian Heap, the Master of St Edmund's College, Cambridge and the many staff and Fellows at the college, especially Dr Brian Stanley, Director of the Henry Martyn Centre. I must also give warm thanks to Dr Philip Towle and Professor James Mayall, successive Directors of the Centre for International Studies of Cambridge University for providing me with a splendid eighteenth-century room in which to work. Graham Howes and Linda Fisher of the University's Board of Continuing Education have been more than encouraging, showing much kindness and intellectual support, as well as giving me plenty of intelligent pupils to teach. I am also most thankful to their equivalents at the University of Richmond's School of Continuing Studies in Virginia, David Kitchen, Cheryl Callaghan and Pat Brown and to Michele Cox and Krittika Onsanit of their International Education Department.

I have also benefited enormously from being a Rockefeller Fellow at the University of Virginia's Foundation for the Humanities' Institute on Violence and Survival. My warmest thanks go here to the Foundation's Director Rob Vaughan, the Institute's Director Roberta Culbertson, and to my old friend and academic colleague, Professor A. E. Dick Howard of the University Law School, who was instrumental in getting me the Fellowship.

I have also been for some years an Annual Writer in Residence at the University of Richmond's History Department – warmest gratitude here goes to my old friend Professor John Treadway, and to the Chairman of the Department, Professor Hugh West. The facilities that they give visiting academics are incomparable.

I would also like to thank that delightful and quintessentially Cambridge couple Professor Geoffrey Williams and his wife Janice, for giving me an annual supply of friendly and intelligent American pupils to teach. They keep many a writer in funds and for that and their cheery encouragement I am most grateful.

I am also indebted, as are all who write on the history of Christianity in the USA, to Professor Mark Noll, of Wheaton College, Illinois, whose many books on this subject are an inspiration. Although my Christian mentor of my student days, Francis Schaeffer, did not always agree with Professor Noll, I am profoundly grateful to the late Dr Schaeffer for introducing me to so many of the themes of this work and for helping me to think in a biblically informed way.

Here I should also thank my late maternal grandfather, Dr D. Martyn Lloyd-Jones, for beginning my love of history and for a spiritual debt of gratitude beyond measure.

As always, I should say that the conclusions I have reached in this book have been my own.

This being a Christian book, I must give profound thanks to

all the staff at the Round Church at St Andrew the Great, the church which my wife and I are privileged to attend. Much gratitude is due to the Vicar, Mark Ashton and to the stalwart members of our Home Group Bible Study, Richard and Sally Reynolds, Will and Corinna Powell and Eric Clouston, who have prayed that this book get finally finished!

Much gratitude for their unstinting moral support also goes to my parents Fred and Elizabeth Catherwood, and to my father-in-law John Moore. For many years the issues discussed in this book have been of enormous interest to them and their encouragement has been invaluable. In particular I thank my mother for her valuable critical insights and comments on the original text of this book.

The University Library in Cambridge has provided more books than I could imagine possible and a great environment in which to work.

Final thanks goes to all the people on my prayer e-mail, who have been so assiduous and kind in praying for me during the writing process. They may not agree with all I have written, but their prayerful support has been of great help in the finishing of this book.

Christopher Catherwood
Cambridge, England
Richmond and Charlottesville, Virginia
September 2002

Prologue:
What This Book Is All About

When someone saw an early draft of this book, she made an interesting observation: 'You talk about nationalism, and then you talk about the way in which Christians in Britain and the USA want to introduce specifically Christian legislation in their respective countries. I don't quite get the link between the two.' My aim is to explain that link.

FROM KOSOVO TO THE FOUNDING OF AMERICA

As we progress, we will be dealing with subjects as diverse as ethnic cleansing in the Balkans and whether or not there were Evangelical Christians among the founders of the American constitution. At a superficial glance these might seem totally separate and not at all linked, in the way that puzzled my questioner above. One of the things I want to achieve in this book is to show that in fact there is such a link, and that we are describing not completely divergent phenomena but degrees of difference of the same thing.

This common thread is the way in which professing Christians mythologize their past in a way that affects their present. In particular, it is the way in which we (for I too am a Christian) attribute the special blessing of God to our own country, to the geographical entity in which we live. This is the case with the Serb reverence for what they regard as the sacred soil of Kosovo, the English habit of regarding God as an Englishman or the American belief that the United States is a city shining upon a hill that is especially blessed by God.

All these tendencies have powerful ramifications in our own

day. The war in Kosovo in 1999, when the Serbs fought to maintain an area that is ethnically overwhelmingly Albanian, is one example, albeit at the extreme end of the scale. English Christians on this side of the Atlantic and our American cousins on the other have the same tendency to regard their own country as somehow exceptional. This has political consequences that are especially pronounced in the USA, as American Christians have a very powerful voice in the political affairs of their nation.

OUR CITIZENSHIP IS IN HEAVEN

What this book aims to show is that as Christians our *prime* loyalty should not be with a political/geographical location called a country, but with the worldwide, multinational, transcultural, interracial body established by Jesus when he was here on earth: the Christian Church. Our citizenship, as the Bible describes it, is in heaven and that is where our principal identity should lie, not with that of the particular country in which we happen to be born.

That is not to ignore the scriptural mandate to be salt and light wherever we find ourselves. Nor is it to ignore the biblical teaching that we are to obey the civil authorities – provided that such obedience does not clash with our higher duty to God. But it is to say that since the coming of Christ, God's people on earth is no longer an ethnic entity or particular country, but the worldwide fellowship of all believers drawn from all racial, ethnic and national groups.

One of the greatest curses of the century we have just left behind was nationalism. Over fifty-five million people died as a result of the Second World War alone. When we look at that kind of nationalist destruction, we are among the first to denounce it. But what is worrying is that many Christians in places such as Britain or the United States are, in their own way, just as nationalist, and fail completely to see the same tendency in themselves. Not only that, but they often spiritualize their prejudices, believing that God is especially blessing their country, an idea which is completely alien to the teaching of the New Testament.

So after a brief introduction, I will look first at the secular phenomenon of nationalism, and then at what the Bible says about the nature of the Christian Church. The final chapters will examine the way in which a false, spiritualized nationalism has infected the Church in both Britain and the United States, the two countries with which I am most familiar. I shall try to show that it is with God's people worldwide that we ought, as Christians, to identify.

1

Looking for Eden

One of the most famous paintings in the world is the impression-ist artist Paul Gauguin's master-work: *Where do we come from? Who are we? Where are we going?* Painted in 1897, and now in the Museum of Fine Arts in Boston, a description of the picture says that it 'expresses the eternal questionings of humans; its ambigui-ties leave it up to the viewer to find the answers'.

It is surely significant that Gauguin painted the picture in Tahiti, a place long thought of by Europeans as akin to paradise. The Book of Genesis tells us that we have been expelled as a human race from the paradise in which we first lived, and there is a real sense in which humanity has been looking for a substitute paradise ever since.

Jesus came to give the answer to the question posed by Gauguin and many like him over the millennia. Where do we come from or, to put it another way, where do we belong? Who are we – what is our true identity? Where are we going – what is our ultimate fate going to be?

This book aims to show what answers Christianity has given to these vital and very basic human longings. In particular I want to examine one uniquely powerful false answer that humanity has come up with over the centuries – that of *nationalism*.

We have, in a sense, created our own false Eden, a myth that in the twentieth century resulted in the deaths of tens of millions in nationalist-induced wars and which threatens the world still.

Many Christians also have fallen for the siren claims of nationalism, the doctrine that the main thing that identifies you as a person is the nation and ethnic group to which you belong by accident of birth.

Can we say that our country, as a political and geographic enti-ty, is a place peculiarly blessed by God? Is that even a legitimate sentiment now that Christ has established a Church here on earth drawn from every nation and race? If the main distinction, since Calvary, is between the saved and the unsaved, what relevance to *Christians* do national boundaries now possess? If God's people now consist of those who profess the name of Christ worldwide, how can we talk of God blessing an individual country when his people, the Church, are spread across the globe?

JESUS IN GLASTONBURY AND OTHER LEGENDS

Women's Institutes in Britain often sing 'Jerusalem', by the poet William Blake (1757–1827). Among the words are to be found the famous lines:

> And did those feet in ancient time
> Walk upon England's mountains green?
> And was the holy Lamb of God
> On England's pleasant pastures seen?
>
> And did the countenance divine
> Shine forth upon our clouded hills?
> And was Jerusalem builded here
> Among those dark satanic mills?

Historically, the notion that Christ or Joseph of Arimathea ever came to Britain is surely risible – and the same would apply to the mythic link with Glastonbury, in the west of England. Probably the majority of women singing the refrain do not believe the myth of Jesus coming to Britain either.

But one could equally argue that the result of the myth is that while twenty-first-century Britons disbelieve it literally, they *do* believe something similar metaphorically, namely that Britain, and England in particular, does have a special place in the purposes of God.

In this, they are not alone. People in many different countries believe that God is with them in some special way or another. As one wag said during the First World War, with both sides claiming that God was on *their* side, he thought it legitimate to ask who was on God's side.

During the epidemic of foot-and-mouth disease in 2001, many asked if this was a judgement of God upon the nation. Like the former Chinese Premier, Zhou Enlai, who, when asked to comment on the French Revolution of (then) over 150 years before, said it was too soon to say, I too felt that such commentary was perhaps premature. Why, too, does one only ask such a question when the countryside is devastated? When Britain's coal, steel and other manufacturing bases were equally badly affected in the 1980s, with a far greater loss of jobs, did no one ask the same question? Is it because rural Britain – like its American heartland equivalent – is seen as more inexorably linked to national identity than the towns in which most people live?

Not long before the foot-and-mouth epidemic in 2001 some parts of the Third World had suffered far greater ecological damage, in floods and other natural disasters. Did this mean that God was judging, say, Mozambique and Bangladesh in an especially severe way? We could all think of countries which are far more anti-Christian or immoral than these two, but which have never been affected by such catastrophes.

To what extent, then, does God speak to nations *as such* in our day?

11 SEPTEMBER 2001

While most present-day Americans have long since rejected the firm faith and biblical perspective of the Pilgrim Fathers, they believe nonetheless that theirs is somehow still a very special nation.

I had the experience of being in Virginia on 11 September 2001. While some Christian leaders did suggest that the terrible tragedy on that day was a good reason for sober national reflection, others did not hesitate to bang the patriotic drum and wrap God and flag very firmly together.

Some leaders, such as Jerry Falwell, blamed the secular

humanists in their midst, and then had to withdraw such massively controversial statements very quickly. Other church leaders pointed out that in the Old Testament, judgement began with the household of God – with believers – rather than with the pagans in whose midst they lived. What was God saying to the *Church* through the carnage of the Pentagon and World Trade Center? Yet others still, with whom I found much affinity, said that such instant judgements were rash, and that the purposes of God would take far longer to fathom.

SO IS THERE SUCH A THING AS A CHRISTIAN COUNTRY?

Can we even say that there is such a thing at all as a Christian country? Are we allowing what are, in reality, secular feelings of nationalism to influence our view of ourselves as God's people here on earth?

Before we get on to such weighty matters, we need to ask: What is the teaching of the Old and New Testaments on the link between a nation and the people of God? In particular, how has it altered since the creation of the Church in the first century? What is the Church? Does an English Christian have more in common with an atheist next-door neighbour than with, say, a fellow Christian in Bangladesh whom he has never met?

When I look at myself in the mirror, what is the most important thing that I see? A proud patriotic Briton/American (delete or substitute as appropriate!), or a child of God rescued by Christ at Calvary? Is there in fact a conflict between these two forms of identity, or are they entirely compatible one with another?

THE LAST REFUGE OF THE SCOUNDREL?

We then need to go on to ask: What is nationalism? Can we legitimately distinguish it from *patriotism*, as many Western Christians seem to do, or is patriotism, simply a less extreme version of a phenomenon that has killed tens of millions of people in the century that we have just left behind?

Above all, perhaps, we need to look at where our loyalties lie, and at the possible conflict of loyalty between the allegiance we owe to God and that which God commands us to have towards the state in which we find ourselves. Countless Christians over the millennia, from the early Church right up to the present, have been martyred because it was God to whom they felt they owed *ultimate* allegiance, and not any transient nation state.

Patriotism, as the great eighteenth-century polymath Dr Johnson once said, is the last refuge of the scoundrel. Can one perhaps say that in our own time nationalism has become a substitute religion for those who have forgotten the true faith, in Jesus Christ?

In the 1930s the crowds adored Hitler, and the Nazis tried to seduce people from Christianity to a faith based upon blood descent and racial superiority. In the 1990s, many Serbian irregular forces murdered their Muslim neighbours in the name of protecting Europe against an Islamic onslaught. In a less violent but still disturbing way, in 2002 in the Presidential elections in France the far-right candidate Jean-Marie Le Pen used the myth of Joan of Arc to stir up hatred against the country's racial and religious minorities. In the USA, links were found between the Oklahoma bomber Timothy McVeigh and extremist white supremacist groups claiming Christian motivation for their views.

So are we as Christians more influenced by secular world-views and ideologies than we care to admit? How much of our thinking is based not upon Scripture but on false Edens, nationalist myths that have no biblical justification?

2

Nationalism: What It Is and Why It Matters

Of theories of nationalism, there is no end. It is a subject that provokes as much controversy in the academic world as nationalist sentiments do in the wider world. Most of us have a view on nationalism, whether or not we have put it into words or explored it in any depth. First of all, we need to define what nationalism is, and then go on to examine where it might originate. Later in this book we will look at specific national myths, and see that some are far less harmful than others.

In our own lifetime, and in that of our grandparents, people have slaughtered each other in the name of nationalist myths, and have invoked the name of Christ on their side to justify their massacres. We might claim that we would never do such things, but we shall see that there is only really a degree of difference in what we believe and what such people do. As Jesus taught us, we may not have committed murder, but we have hated and that too is a sin. None of us is truly innocent.

PATRIOTS AND NATIONALISTS?

I am a patriot – you are a nationalist!

As Christ's parable of the mote and the beam (or the speck and the log) reminds us, it is very easy to condemn others and be guilty of the same sin in an even worse way ourselves. In both World Wars, perhaps more in the First World War than in the Second, Christians on both sides eagerly prayed for victory. Clearly these prayers were incompatible! But patriotic Britons and patriotic Germans both believed that God was on *their* side and not that of their national enemy.

In the Second World War, many devout German Christians, such as Bonhoeffer and the members of the Kreisau Circle, decided that Hitler was so evil that Christianity had to come before German patriotism, a very brave decision that cost many of them their lives at the hands of the Nazis. In Britain there were Christians, like Bishop Bell of Chichester, who were criticized for being opposed to bombing, but there were no vocal British Christians keenly praying for an Axis victory.

Politicians are often accused of 'wrapping themselves in the flag'. Yet Christians, especially in Western democracies such as Britain or the United States, often believe that patriotism really is a virtue. They distinguish it from nationalism, which they would agree is a bad thing, and is of course always believed in by people from other countries, like the French.

I am going to argue, by contrast, that patriotism and nationalism are really only two degrees of the same thing. In this chapter we will consider the secular phenomenon, and in the next one we will see what the Bible has to say about the subject. Eventually I shall come to the conclusion that as Christians our citizenship is in heaven, as Scripture teaches, not here on earth. We are commanded to obey our earthly rulers, but our loyalty *must* lie elsewhere.

A QUESTION OF SELF-IDENTITY: WHO WE ARE AND WHERE OUR LOYALTIES LIE

Who are we? Why are patriotism and nationalism like hate and murder? In order to find out we must first look at the issue of *self-identity*: who we are and why the way we think of ourselves is important, both as citizens of our country and as Christians living in a fallen world.

Let us start with *national* self-identity, and then go on to look at other self-identities. We all have many self-identities, for different parts of our lives, though some are more important to us than others.

I am married to Paulette, a Virginian. I am Scotch Irish (or

Ulster Scottish) on one side of the family, and Welsh on the other. By genetic ancestry, I am all the components of the United Kingdom except English. However, some of my family say that as I have lived in England all my life, it is pedantic to say that I am *not* English. My fervently Celtic family upbringing is cancelled out, or certainly equalled, by the English culture that I have inhabited for nearly fifty years.

So what am I? British? English? Since devolution for Scotland and Wales in 1999, this has become a major subject not just of academic debate but of discussion in pubs, football clubs and many other normal venues of life besides. *Englishness* has suddenly come back into vogue, with the specifically English flag of St George now often replacing the Union Jack as a symbol of patriotic pride.

I have always felt myself to be simply *British*. Since that neatly includes England in its remit, it solves the problem for me as an individual as to what I am. I am a Celtic Scottish Irish Welshman raised in England – all four segments of the United Kingdom rolled into one.

Mongrels like me, while common in the USA, are, however, comparatively rare in Britain. Most people would think of themselves as being only one of the components. Genetically, they would probably be wrong to do so. DNA research on the English shows that a very large percentage of them have Celtic genes. The pre-Saxon-invasion Celtic minority was not all massacred or pushed to the fringes of Wales and Cornwall. There was a lot of intermarriage between invaders and conquered, and the English race of today is the result. Similarly the Viking invasions brought much Scandinavian blood into the English gene pool. Last, some DNA archaeology has discovered that some Britons have black, North African slave ancestry in their genes, which came over with Roman slaves in the early centuries of the Christian era. So many a pure-bred Englishman has plenty of Welsh, Danish and North African blood in his veins.

Similarly, if you ask my wife what she is, she would reply that she is a Virginian. Only secondarily would she say that she is an American. She has all four components of Britishness, laced with a smattering of Choctaw Native American blood.

A TYPICAL WELSHMAN . . . SHE IS *SO* CALIFORNIAN . . .

'Taffy was a Welshman, Taffy was a thief.' 'California – that's where the fruits and nuts come from.'

One Christian pamphlet on national identity, published not too long ago, began by saying that we all laugh at a good Irish joke. (Being partly Irish I only find them partly funny.) Humour is always a helpful thing, and the true sign of a real sense of humour is surely that you can laugh at yourself as well as at the misfortunes or quirks of others. But are ethnic jokes legitimate, even if it is a Jewish mother-in-law joke told by Brooklyn Jewish comedians? More to the point, are they *accurate*?

A reason why many Virginians call themselves such is to distinguish what they regard as noble Virginian characteristics, style and culture from brash New Yorkers or flaky Californians. Virginians know the difference, but people from other countries may not. (How often have we said, 'Oh, you're from New York – maybe you know my friends in Los Angeles,' when those two cities are thousands of miles apart.) Likewise, a gritty Yorkshireman would not want to be confused with some wimpish southerner from the Home Counties, or a *latte*-drinking denizen of Islington with some boorish culturally illiterate oik from the North.

If these stereotypes have caused your blood to boil, I can assuage your wrath by saying that they should have! Christians are, alas, as prone to this kind of woolly thinking as the people around them. Yet how often have we gone to a church in a quite different part of the country and found that we get on really well with the people there. Not only are they completely unlike the stereotypes but we are surprised at how much we find in common with them.

People who have ventured beyond the parameters of Disney World often discover that culturally different parts of the USA are quite distinct. Our idea that 'all Americans are alike' turns out not to be true at all. California and Virginia *are* unalike. We realize that to lump all Americans together is mistaken, and that when we did so in the past we were acting out of ignorance.

Perhaps we realize this most when we are the victims. I have been to some parts of Europe, with friends from the countries in question, and have been told by them to keep my British identity quiet. British lager louts and football hooligans have created a terrible reputation for their home country worldwide. During the 2000 World Cup, Scottish football fans were at pains to ensure that their French hosts knew that they were from civilized Scotland and not violence-prone England. Yet most English people would be among the first to condemn the mindless violence of a small minority of fans, and regard the way in which everyone from England is tarred with their brush as being most unfair. To which I would reply that it is unfair. But in Britain we do the same thing all the time to other countries. How often do we say 'the French!' or worse still 'the Krauts!'

THE MANY IDENTITIES OF A FOOTBALL FAN

The well-known historian Norman Davies, in his book *The Isles*, has used the football analogy to talk about the thorny issue of national characteristics. I will be adapting his ideas to fit in with the purposes of this book.

Let us imagine three football supporters: Ahmed who supports Leeds, Winston who follows West Ham and Dave who roots for Chelsea.

All three of them have something in common – a love of soccer. However, they support different teams, and this divides them, especially if their respective sides are playing each other. All of them are British, born in England. Ahmed is of Pakistani origin, Winston is of Afro-Caribbean descent and Dave is English.

Ahmed, though, is from Yorkshire, so is a northerner. Dave and Winston are both from London, and in one sense can thus be described as southerners. However, in Yorkshire, Ahmed is from the South Asian community as well as being a northerner – he might support Leeds in football and Yorkshire in cricket, but to the racists in the north of England who were involved in riots in 2001, he is a foreigner, a 'Paki'. This is despite the fact that he is Yorkshire born as they are, and as avid a supporter of their favourite sports teams as they are.

Similarly, Winston's grandparents came from the Caribbean, though he himself was born in London and his parents were children when they migrated to England. However, his grand-parents were from Barbados. This means that they are *not* Jamaicans, something of which, in their own community, they are very proud. The whole family is cricket mad, and while Winston supports West Ham in football, he supports the West Indies in cricket, and is proud of the fact that they are one of the best teams in the world.

Dave is pure Anglo-Saxon in descent, so far as he knows. He and Winston have been friends since childhood, because they go to school together. In Brixton, where they both live, Dave is the one in a minority, since the area is heavily Afro-Caribbean. In London as a whole, however, Dave is in the majority.

When Leeds plays West Ham or Chelsea, Ahmed is on the opposing side to the other two. But when the England football team played Germany, all three fans were in the England stands, rooting for the home team. Although all three support the England football team, only Dave would consider himself English.

Ahmed and Winston come from stable family backgrounds; Dave does not. Ahmed is expected to do well at school, go to university and be a prosperous member of the middle class. Winston's family is tight knit, and his parents wondered about sending him to school in Barbados, as the crime rate is much lower than in Brixton, and the children have traditional respect for their teachers. Dave's family have all left school by the age of sixteen, and his older brother is permanently in trouble with the police.

When the three of them went on holiday in Spain, the locals disliked them because they were seen as 'Brits', liable to get drunk, have fights and wreck their rooms. The hotel staff were in fact surprised to find all of them well-mannered, polite and friendly.

Traditionally in beach resorts, the British regard the Germans as their great rivals, despite the fact that Germany has been at peace with Britain for over fifty years, and is a close NATO and EU ally. Our three Britons teased the German youths, but stopped short when they saw one of them, Günther, wearing a cross around his neck. Yes, Günther told them, he was a Christian. This transformed the situation.

For Ahmed was converted through the former Mission to Asians in Britain. He now attends an Anglican youth group in Bradford, which makes his Muslim parents sad, but resigned, because at least the Church of England is respectable. Winston has long been a keen member of his local New Testament Church of God, an Afro-Caribbean denomination. Dave became a Christian through an outreach group of Ichthus, a large house church that is Pentecostal in style. All three of their churches are part of the Evangelical Alliance. Günther attends a Lutheran church at home, and is part of the interdenominational Christian student group, the *Studentenmission in Deutschland*, a key member of the International Fellowship of Evangelical Students (IFES). So all four are professing Evangelical Christians.

None of them is Baptist, but on Sunday they find that the only Protestant Church is a Spanish-speaking Baptist church. Knowing no Spanish themselves, they try it out with trepidation. To their surprise, they discover that they receive a warm welcome, especially by the other teenagers in the church. 'Isn't it great,' the pastor says, in faulty English, 'that although we have never met before, we are all brothers and sisters in Christ together.'

PRIMARY AND SECONDARY FORMS OF SELF-IDENTITY

What we have just read is a story, although much of it is true to my experience. I attended many IFES international student conferences back in the 1970s and 1980s. We came from literally all over the world, and most of us had never met before. Yet we found an enormous sense of kinship, since we had so much in common. We were all students, and of similar age, and that, of course, brought us closely together. Watch the interaction at many a youth hostel in a big tourist city and you will see something similar.

However, what really united us was that we had the most important possible thing of all in common – our shared Christian faith. We will look at this in more detail in the next chapter, when we consider what the Apostle Paul had to say about such things in his epistles. But we certainly found his writings to be true in practice for us. I will never forget seeing Jewish Christian students from Israel embracing Arab Christian students from Egypt on a conference platform – there was not a dry eye in the auditorium. Many of the students at that conference did not speak English as a common language, but they did not need to. What they could see on stage was demonstration enough of Christian unity.

As the illustration of the football fan trio demonstrates, we all have different identities at different times and points in our lives. We are our parents' children, someone's neighbour, another person's colleague at work, our spouse's other half, a member of the local church, a supporter of a particular sports team, a citizen of our country and many other things besides.

THE MANY FACES OF YOUR AUTHOR

If you take your author as an example: I am, as I said, British but not English. I am one of the minority who was privately educated, not at a state school – with the sad consequence that many judge me for my accent without knowing that I hate social snobbery in all its forms. I went to Oxford University (which some say is very elitist), but to Balliol College, where privately educated pupils were only a tiny proportion of the student body. Being a member of the Labour Party put me on the far right wing, since Maoists and Trotskyites abounded. Fully one-third of the student body was from overseas, many from the Third World. The Master of the

College was a Marxist, but he liked Evangelicals, since he was a specialist on the seventeenth-century Puritans and recognized our theological kinship with them.

As I mentioned earlier, I am part of an Anglo-American marriage. I am also an historian, based in Cambridge, and have a loose affiliation to a graduate college, St Edmund's, that has as cosmopolitan and international an atmosphere as the Balliol of my youth. This means that I now win and lose the famous Boat Race every year. I am now middle-aged and do not have as much hair on my head as I used to. So in terms of the 'postmodern personal narrative discourse' so popular in universities today, that makes me a *cosmopolitan*.

Here I should add that being an Evangelical who believes in absolute truth, I am no postmodernist – but as all that is not the subject of this book, I can refer you to the excellent works of N. T. Wright, published by SPCK, should you wish to delve deeper.

Some of my cosmopolitan background is cultural. London is an international city and the borough in which I was raised had large Polish and South Asian communities. But much of this was also Christian. My childhood church, Westminster Chapel, in those days was one of the world's best-known churches, with a very large congregation drawn from all over the world. Its minister, my maternal grandfather, D. Martyn Lloyd-Jones, was also one of the founders of the International Fellowship of Evangelical Students, so family living rooms were regularly full of people from every country imaginable.

My grandfather also helped to found IFES in an interesting way, in that it was designed to have indigenous, not Western missionary, leadership from the very beginning. This meant that when some of the member movements suddenly found themselves, in the late 1940s, under Communist rule, the leaders could continue while all the foreign missionaries were expelled. Dr Lloyd-Jones's Welsh roots under what he regarded as English colonial rule also gave him a natural empathy with colonial peoples!

From an early age, therefore, I knew instinctively, as John Stott has since written, that Christianity is *transcultural*. We will look at this later, but in terms of personal narrative it was something I experienced from childhood and then discovered, on becoming a Christian, that it was *absolutely* true, in the biblical sense, as well.

BRITAIN AND THE COMPLEXITIES OF MULTIPLE IDENTITY

In Britain we are now seeing the sad phenomenon of black-on-black violence, which is quite often gangs of Afro-Caribbean teenagers setting upon children of direct African ancestry – whose families are immigrants from places such as Nigeria and Ghana. This is because Africans are keen on the united family, hard work and high achievement. Although, like the imaginary Winston, those in strong Christian homes in the Afro-Caribbean community have an equally strong sense of family and ambition, the destruction by white slave owners over many centuries did lasting damage to the sense of familial unity and self-image of their slaves' descendants.

In the USA, those from Caribbean backgrounds, like General Colin Powell, are regarded as high achievers compared with the mainstream African-American community; many of the latter have the social and identity problems that are associated in Britain with the Afro-Caribbean community.

In Britain, children of Nigerian ancestry who get high marks and go on to university are seen, in a perverse way, as letting the side down and being like the hated white man. Again, this is ironic, since in the Caribbean countries of origin, while the nuclear family is sometimes missing (usually because the father is absent), wider family ties are strong and learning is held in high esteem.

So when white racists speak about 'black' people, they do so in ignorance as well as in hatred. Black self-identity is thoroughly mixed, with many Trinidadians coming from a culture of inter-ethnic mixing and often tolerance, and the cultures of several other Caribbean islands being socially very conservative. Also many a Kenyan or Ghanaian will tell you that they are not Nigerians, in the same way that a Lancastrian will let you know that while they may be a northerner, they are most certainly not from Yorkshire! Nigerians regard these stereotypes as unfair, as do Americans in relation to European caricatures.

Furthermore, all these different ethnic groups, while they may have different ancestral cultures, are, as time progresses, becoming an integral part of the warp and woof of what being British is all about. A few years back, a Scottish politician got in trouble with some segments of society for saying that chicken tikka masala was as much a British dish today as more traditional English fare. While some protested, I think he is right.

Not only that: my Welsh relations have the perfect response to those who say that the 'West Indians', Pakistanis and others should go back to their 'home' country. They will agree to that only if the English return to Lower Saxony in Germany and to Jutland in Denmark where they belong. All the English are immigrants, after all!

SO WHAT IS ENGLISH PATRIOTISM ALL ABOUT?

Given that Britain, with England included, is now such a multi-cultural and polyglot society, one does wonder what English patriotism is properly all about. Most English people themselves do not live in quaint villages with thatched cottages, cricket being played on the green and rustics drinking real ale at an ancient pub.

Later on in this book, we will look at some specific countries, and see how their religious mythologies have created a false vision of paradise. Here we will first look at the concept behind the phenomenon. This has been called *palingenetics* or myth-based ultra-nationalism. It is a term popularized by Roger Griffin, a specialist on fascism. In using the term himself, though, Griffin feels that fascism is *not* something quasi-religious, whereas I have argued (in my book *Why the Nations Rage*) that it can be, in some circumstances.

In this book we are looking at the myths and longings for an idyllic past that form a basis for our national self-identity. In our examination of this myth-based view of our origins, I think that palingenetics is an ideal tool for understanding them, and that the phenomenon we are studying is something specifically religious.

Let us look at the three components of palingenetics: *myth-based*, *ultra* and *nationalism*.

MYTHS OF BELONGING: AMERICA AND THE MYTH OF
THE EMPTY WILDERNESS

First of all, we need a myth, something far in the distant past, to which we can all look back with longing.

Those who have studied native peoples, or ancient societies, know that such groups have what they call *creation myths* – stories of how their group of people came into being. However, what we forget in the West is that we have very similar myths ourselves, but we give 'people groups' different names – we refer to African *tribes*, for example, but *ethnic minority groups* here in Europe. Sociologists are surely right when they refer to groups of football supporters as 'tribes' of people who follow a particular team!

Let us look at stories familiar to English-speaking readers, so that we can get a general, initial idea of the subject matter.

In the USA there is the frontier myth of brave people going out to settle virgin territory, battling against nature and hostile Indians. Many of the social attitudes of present-day Americans, with their 'can-do' image, are attributable to the pioneer spirit they feel that they inherit from their ancestors.

However, in many cases, the ancestors of current Americans arrived in North America a long time after the frontier was settled, and society had become more sedentary. Far more important, the virgin lands occupied by the earlier pioneers had in fact been settled for thousands of years by the peoples that we now call Native Americans. Their ancestors had come over the Bering Straits from Asia millennia before any white European had ever even heard that the continents of North and South America existed.

The frontier myth of the USA is exactly that – a myth. Much of it is, though, based on truth – there were brave Europeans who, hundreds of years ago, blazed a trail in parts of the world where no one of European ancestry had been before. While they were not the first humans ever to have inhabited such a territory, the conditions were harsh, and survival was not easy. We shall also see later how the settlers added a specifically religious component to their occupation of the continent.

CREATION MYTHS AND THE NATIVE AMERICANS

Native Americans of many different groupings had their creation myths, far older than many in Europe, which were based upon ancient oral traditions going back possibly thousands of years.

Nowadays, because of the high regard in which Native American peoples are said to view nature, these myths are regarded with some awe. They are very similar to creation stories around the world, held by ethnic groups with the same pre-European-contact degrees of literacy. In that sense they are not unlike the tales of ancient Greece, or of the Egyptian contemporaries of the Children of Israel.

If we look at them not ecologically but as folk memory, a pre-literate way of describing how their ancestors got physically to where they are today, the Native American creation myths make much more sense. But although there is less remaining factual basis in them than, say, the tales of the wagon trail out West by Europeans, their basic import is the same. They are a means of saying 'we are here and we are special'.

In the nineteenth century, as anyone who watches 'cowboy and Indian' films will remember, there was much blood spilt between the whites of European descent and the Native Americans. Both felt that they had the right to be where they were. Today, such films or TV series would not be made, since we understand that what happened then was a form of ethnic cleansing, or even genocide. White Americans who might have unpleasantly racist attitudes to African Americans are often proud of having some Native American blood, especially if it proves some link to a famous example such as Pocahontas or Sitting Bull. Films such as *Dances with Wolves* show how susceptibilities have changed: while the massacre of the heroine's family and her kidnapping are not glossed over, the basic sympathy towards the Native Americans is very clear.

Thankfully those days of violent conflict are over, although Native Americans still, for the most part, live hundreds of miles away from their ancestral dwelling grounds. The legacy of the notorious *Trail of Tears* is still with us.

But much of the mythology, both of white and Native American, lives on, albeit now in more peaceful form. I have seen many a superbly laid out museum detailing the lives of the early European settlers, from Virginia to Missouri. While such places give the original inhabitants of the USA their full due, there is also a strong sense of pride in what the first Europeans were able to achieve, often against the fiercest of natural obstacles in environmentally difficult terrain.

Paradoxically, now that the unpleasant aspects – the effective ethnic cleansing of Native Americans from their original home-lands – are no longer glossed over or even glorified, the sheer impressiveness of the European settler achievements in all other respects can be seen more clearly. Since many museums recreate the original living quarters in exact detail, often with hardy volunteers actually living in them year round, one can see how harsh their conditions were. While their European countries of origin were not bursting with amenities either, the fact that England or southern Germany were advanced countries of ancient settlement meant that the home environment was physically much more secure, the climate far more familiar, even if the political or religious atmosphere was hostile. The frontier people had to be formidable to survive the first winter, let alone a lifetime in the New World.

The frontier myth is thus something understandably potent

and, combined with its religious counterpart, it has a major resonance in the USA today. Likewise, one can argue that the powerful creation myths of the Native American peoples have enabled them to survive the semi-genocide and massive upheavals inflicted upon their ancestors in the nineteenth century.

But terrible though the fate of Native Americans was in the era of Custer and Sitting Bull, it was to be overshadowed by the fifty-five million or more people who died as a result of the Second World War.

ULTRA-NATIONALISM: THE MYTHS GET NASTY

Here we come to the other parts of palingenetics: *ultra-nationalism*.

Nationalism, as I argued earlier in this chapter, is always *potentially* dangerous because of the extremes to which it can lead. For Europeans, and for Americans who possess a heightened sense of global awareness (especially since 11 September 2001), few events have been as worrying as the evident resurgence of racist nationalism in 2002.

One of the most telling photographs of the French National Front leader Jean-Marie Le Pen was in front of a statue of Joan of Arc in Orleans. As the press made clear, Joan has become almost a patron saint of Le Pen's party. Joan has long been a symbol of France. Although there has long been a country of that name, it was not until the fifteenth century that there was truly a single country under the rule of the King of France. If you remember the history of Henry II of England, you will recall that he ruled over far more of France than did the poor French king, whose direct authority extended to not much more than the area around Paris itself. Although subsequent kings were able to extend their territory, it was not until Joan of Arc's time, the fifteenth century, that the French were able to expel the English from their domains (except Calais) and be Kings of France in reality as well as in name.

However, as we saw in 2002, Joan of Arc, hitherto a symbol of all of France, has now in effect been hijacked by an extremist ultra-nationalist party, the National Front, who are using her name and the patriotic myth that surrounds her for their own political purposes. (I think one can use the term *myth* for Joan, since, although she was a real person, her 'voices' and claims of divine aid cannot be scientifically measured for accuracy.) A symbol that all could claim is now being used by those who have a very narrow, xenophobic view of who is and who is not French. The myth of a unified France is now being exploited by those whose national vision is divisive and exclusive rather than inclusive.

Since the time of the French Revolution, French citizens have been defined as those born within the geographic boundaries of the French state. Whatever Napoleon's many faults, racial prejudice was not among them – few people have done more to make Jews into equal citizens alongside the gentile majority around them. To Le Pen and his associates, though, being born in France no longer makes you French. He has restored the anti-Semitism that came to the fore in France at the end of the nineteenth century in what is now called the Dreyfus Affair, when a French Jewish officer was wrongly accused of treason and sent to Devil's Island. This was an ugly phenomenon that reached its apogee in the Second World War in the part of France ruled by French collaborationists with the Nazis in the Vichy Republic. Le Pen is also virulently Islamophobic, wanting to expel the nine million or so French citizens of Muslim faith (and usually of North African racial origin), even though most of that group were born in France itself.

One of the things that has emerged in France in recent years is the very large extent of willing collaboration with the Nazis in Vichy times. Le Pen and his beliefs are in no small measure a revival of that racist, fascist tradition. In his version of France, you don't just have to be born there to be truly French – the old *cosmopolitan* racially inclusive sense of national identity – but to be ethnically French as well. This is why genetically non-French groups, whether Jewish or North African, are no longer welcome.

Until recently Germany had a similar version of what it meant to be truly German – something only abandoned in the last few years. In legal terms this is called *jus sanguinis* and *jus solis*, or *law of blood descent* versus *law of place of birth* in rough translation.

THE MELTING-POT IDEA VS 'KEEP THEM OUT!'

A melting-pot country such as the United States is one of *jus solis*. If you are born in the USA, you are an American, whatever your racial or ethnic origin. As should be obvious, that is what makes America what it is: a truly cosmopolitan nation whose citizens come from all quarters of the earth. The USA is a country of immigrants, from those of Asian ancestry who came over the Bering Straits thousands of years ago to the millions who have arrived in more recent years and right up to the present time. There would be no America without immigrants.

To Le Pen and his like, the whole problem is immigration – those not of pure French blood (*sanguinis*) are unwelcome.

In German law until recently, what qualified you for citizenship was German blood. Your ancestors could have left Germany centuries ago, but you today, their remote descendant, are qualified to live there now because of them. This created many twentieth-century absurdities, which is why the Social Democrat/Green coalition abolished the *jus sanguinis*, though not without opposition from those who preferred the old ways.

Germans, or 'Saxons' as they were called, whose ancestors went to live in Transylvania (now in Romania) in the Middle Ages, came back to live in present-day Germany after the fall of Romanian communism in 1989. Other Germans, whose forebears settled in central Russia in the eighteenth century, also returned to Germany, following the collapse of the USSR in 1991. Many of both categories of ethnic German spoke not a word of their ancestral language. Ethnic Turkish young people, however, who had been born in Germany, whose parents had themselves probably also either been born in the country or come there when very young, with *their* parents, were, until very recently, denied German citizenship. This was even though they were the third generation of their family to live and work in the country.

If your right to live in the country comes by being born in it, then the German-born Turks were fully entitled to their citizenship, which many now enjoy. But if it is by blood descent, then those whose ancestors left hundreds of years ago and who had never visited it (because communist governments forbade it), had a better right.

What can be described as a cosmopolitan view of citizenship includes everybody. After 11 September 2001, the American TV networks showed a series of advertisements, with people of every ethnic combination imaginable, all proudly saying to the camera: 'I am an American'. As well as being an ethnic melting pot, the USA is also possibly the most religiously diverse country on earth, with many different mainstream religions and small sects of every description imaginable all living cheek by jowl. One of the founding principles of the country, enshrined in the constitution, is that there is no official religion in the USA. People can believe anything they like, and one only has to look at the religious smorgasbord available to see that this is indeed the case. As anyone who has studied European and American history will remember, many of the settlers in the USA over the centuries have been people fleeing their homeland to go to North America to practise their chosen faith in freedom.

As often as not, the place they left behind is a European country, whether the England of Puritan times, the Holy Roman Empire of the Thirty Years War, or the Jewish-persecuting Tsarist Empire portrayed in films such as *Fiddler on the Roof* or *Yentl*.

EXCLUSIVIST VS INCLUSIVIST WAYS OF LOOKING AT PEOPLE

The key thing for us to grasp here is that ultra-nationalism is exclusivist not inclusivist. In an inclusive country, you are defined positively, by what you are now. Furthermore, you can acquire such a status – you do not have to be born into it or inherit it. Even if you possess not a drop of white Anglo-Saxon Protestant blood, you can become a fully fledged American citizen.

But as we have just seen, in an exclusivist country, if you were not born genetically German, for example, or if you did not have genetically German descent, then citizenship of that country was effectively denied to you, even if you had been born there and your parents before you. And one of the reasons that the Social Democratic/Green coalition government in Germany was able to get rid of the *jus sanguinis* law is that they were able to show that it was a hangover from a far more unpleasant part of German history: the Nazi period.

Nazism is perhaps the ultimate example of palingenetics at work. This is because the Nazis defined people not merely by what they were, but by what they were *not*. Whole swathes of people who were born in Germany and whose ancestors had lived there for centuries, were excluded from what it meant to be a 'true' German. In particular, as we know all too well from the Holocaust, Jews were utterly excluded from the very narrow sense of German-ness proclaimed by the Third Reich. (We will look later on in this book at some more recent and sadly equally murderous examples of palingenetics at work.)

The Nazis did not hesitate to use the symbolism and mythology of ancient, pre-Roman Germany to build up the case for their pathological view of a pure, Teutonic or Aryan, master race. Although a film such as *Raiders of the Lost Ark* is imaginary, there were entirely genuine expeditions, funded by Himmler and the SS, to examine the supposed ancient ethnic origins of the German race and the reasons for their superiority over all others.

For the purposes of this book, what is also frightening is the extent to which so many German Christians did go along with such murderous nonsense. Historiography today is vehemently divided over how many Germans collaborated fully with the Nazi regime and, in particular, whether there was something specifically German about the Holocaust.

There were brave individual Christians who resisted, such as Dietrich Bonhoeffer and the Kreisau Circle. But we also know that there was massive collaboration with the Nazis in all the countries which they occupied (including, British people should always remember, in the Channel Islands, the one part of the United Kingdom occupied by the Germans). I think it is therefore safe to say that the period 1933–45 showed that the *whole* of Europe displayed genocidal racist tendencies, rather than just the Germans in particular.

But non-specialist books and TV series, such as *The Nazis: A Warning from History* and new research on Vichy France, remind us all too clearly that if ordinary everyday people had not collaborated with the SS in Germany or with the occupiers in France, then millions of innocent people – socialists, gypsies and the mentally ill, as well as Jews – would never have died.

While there are countless views of the exact identity of the Antichrist, one thing is certain – he will deceive Christians as well as non-believers. The fact that so many Christians must, in those terrible 12 years, have either done nothing or actually in some way agreed with the perpetrators shows what a danger false teaching is to the Church. As the Christian writer and thinker Francis Schaeffer said on another issue, it is not just the act itself, but that the act is *possible*. It is the fact that ordinary people, many of them professing Christians, think that people from another race are somehow inferior that is the problem. If the average German, Frenchman, Ukrainian or whatever had regarded the Jew next door as no different from himself, then the first step to the Holocaust would never have been taken.

The seventeen per cent scored by Jean-Marie Le Pen in France in 2002, and the twelve per cent achieved by an anti-immigrant party in Denmark, a Protestant country normally regarded as highly tolerant, show that this kind of exclusivist mentality has not gone away.

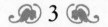

3

How We Got to Where We Are Now: A Quick History Lesson

'I slit the throats of two Turks today and I don't have nightmares.'

This rather blood-curdling boast of a young Serb militia member during the savage Bosnian conflict in the 1990s shows us all too vividly what happens when Christian mythology and mass murder go together. We have looked at nationalism in its different forms, but now need to go on to look at how Christianity and national myth have become tragically enmeshed over the centuries, right up to our own times.

This is going to be the theme of this chapter, and it ought to make sobering reading, as we discover how Christianity, the faith of the Prince of Peace, has been so manipulated and distorted over the centuries, right up to very recent times. We will also see how Christians in comparatively non-violent Western countries are affected, as well as those in areas that we normally associate with conflict. So before we go on to examine the English-speaking world, let us first consider historically how we arrived at the situation in which we are now.

THE PROBLEM OF BEING BRITISH OR AMERICAN

One of the big problems of being British or American is that we think that our kind of patriotism would never lead to anything unpleasant. Consequently, it is perfectly all right for us to be patriotic, and perhaps spiritually patriotic at the same time. After all, are not both Britain and the USA Christian countries, with long-established Christian foundations? Surely it is all right to be proud of our nation and of its Christian heritage at the same time?

The major difficulty with such an approach is that it is not one that can be made on principle, because it has to be country specific. It also ignores factors such as what *actually* happened in history, how Christianity was manipulated for political ends and, most important of all, in the cases of Britain and the USA, the enormous influence of geography upon what happens to a country's fate.

In Britain, we tend readily to forget that our biggest national denomination, the Church of England, began as a result of political expediency, born out of an adulterous king's desire to marry another woman even though he had a lawful wife already. (I deal with all this extensively in my book *Five Leading Reformers*, and to a smaller degree in another work, *A Crash Course on Church History*.) In Scotland it was slightly different – there was a strong grass-roots Protestant movement, which succeeded when a rebellion against the French-dominated Catholic monarchy managed to prevail.

GERMANY: LAND OF THE REFORMATION AND OF
ADOLF HITLER

In Germany, the land of Martin Luther, the Reformation had entirely spiritual beginnings. It is also true that without political support, provided by princes such as the Elector of Saxony or the Landgrave of Hesse, Luther would probably have been martyred like Jan Hus the century before, and thus not ultimately as successful as he turned out to be. But in Germany, unlike England, spiritual desire for reformation preceded the political will to carry it out. In England, scholarship has now shown, a truly Protestant reformation did not in reality get under way until the reign of Edward VI, and there was a long-lasting popular Catholicism in the country until well into the reign of Elizabeth I.

So if a part of Europe (Germany did not exist in a formal sense until 1871) can be said to have a truly glorious *spiritual* heritage, it is Germany and not England. By and large, the parts of Germany that were Protestant in 1648 (the end of the Thirty Years War) have remained so until today, and the same applies to the areas that are still Catholic.

But Germany is also the country of Adolf Hitler and the Nazis. While Protestants do not hesitate to laud the great spiritual achievements of Martin Luther, they neglect the unfortunate fact that when it came to Jews, he was very much a man of his day and place. Anti-Semitism has an ancient history. Anyone reading Sir Walter Scott's novel *Ivanhoe* will know that England was no exception, and it was not until Cromwell's time in the seventeenth century that Jews were allowed back in and not until the nineteenth century that practising Jews were able to vote.

In terms of heritage, therefore, the land that begat the Reformation begat the Holocaust as well. Here it is worth remembering that many German Jews did not flee in time because up until then the really bad instances of anti-Semitism had been in France and Russia. The Habsburg Emperors of Austria, in whose realm Hitler was born, had a long history of protecting Jews against anti-Semitic outrages. But when it came to the 1930s, that Christian heritage clearly did not count for much.

POLITICIAL PROTESTANTISM IN THE BRITISH ISLES

Modern scholarship now emphasizes the way in which Protestantism has played a very significant part in creating the national identity that we have in Britain. Unfortunately, many British Christians, including (and sometimes especially) Evangelicals, whose faith ought to be more scripturally than nationalistically based, have followed this propaganda right up to our very own time. This, I will argue, is a very serious mistake, and for two reasons. First, it does not take account of the reality of the past, and second it utterly fails to understand the actual nature of Christian conversion as understood in the Bible and by the early Church.

One of the most often quoted and highly regarded history books of recent years is *Britons: Forging the Nation 1707–1837* by Linda Colley, formerly living in the USA but now at London University. Professor Colley has not just been read by historians, but has also lectured on the substance of her book to the Prime Minister at 10 Downing Street. In her work, she shows that Protestantism, and the common Protestant identity of England, Scotland and Wales, played a pivotal role in unifying the newly formed Great Britain. She starts in 1707 as that was the year in which Britain became a politically united state for the first time, with the dissolution of the independent Scottish Parliament in Edinburgh. (We did not become the United Kingdom until 1801, when the Irish Parliament was abolished.)

Geography – the fact that all three of these nations shared one island – had not led to unity in the past. Until 1603 Scotland had been not only completely independent and under different rulers, but a country often at war with its more powerful English neighbour to the south. (Even today it often happens that if England plays France at football or rugby, many a Scot will automatically support the French!)

After the Reformation, however, both England and Scotland shared a very strong sense of common Protestant identity, each with a national Protestant established Church, albeit with differing structures and theological emphases. This shared Protestant identity thus became all the more important when the rulers of the new Great Britain sought to forge a common sense of being *British* as opposed to being either English or Scottish.

There is unquestionably much truth in what historians call the Colley thesis. One of the things that most helped in forging a sense of common Protestant Britishness is that most of our enemies on the continent, and above all the French, were Catholic. In particular, since King Louis XIV of France had repealed the Edict of Nantes, the 1598 law that gave French Protestants (or Huguenots) freedom of worship, France was seen not only as the national enemy but also as a state that oppressed and exiled fellow Protestants – much to the economic benefit, it should be said, of countries like Britain that took them in.

WHY DO EVANGELICALS LOOK ON THIS PERIOD
WITH SUCH A GLOW?

Professor Colley is correct in her analysis of the past, but there are some crucial things which we should not overlook.

First of all, it is odd that Evangelical Christians should look back on this period with such a glow. Although the lot of non-conformists was much improved by the Act of Toleration passed after the Glorious Revolution of 1688–9, they did not have full equality with members of the Church of England until over a century later. One of the reasons why the Methodist Revival of the late eighteenth century was so spiritually necessary was that the established Church was so moribund and lacklustre. It is surely not without significance that much of the inspiration for men such as Wesley and Whitefield came from fellow Christians in Germany and over the Atlantic in the American colonies, where the Great Awakening was taking place.

When we think of Jonathan Edwards and other leaders of North American Christianity at this time, we need also to remember the works of another outstanding American preacher, Cotton Mather. His writing makes it very plain that much of the spiritual zeal we associate with the Puritans and other similar settlers in New England had long departed. The extraordinary measure called the 'Half-Way Covenant' was an admission by second- and third-generation Puritans that not all children of Christians in New England were themselves believers. It recognized that many of the descendants of the godly seventeenth-century colonists were no longer anything like as active in or committed to the faith that motivated their ancestors to flee Britain and come to the New World.

In other words, the situation was not as rosy in this period as many Christians now like to think.

Not only that, but Evangelicals, with their strong emphasis on Scripture, should of all people recognize that there is a profound difference between being a citizen of a so-called Christian country, and being a practising, believing Christian. This was one of the most important doctrines that arose as a result of the Reformation. The doctrine of *sola fidei* – by faith alone – made it clear that it was an individual's personal faith, rather than their country of birth, that determined whether or not someone was born again. (I expand on the consequences of this in my book *Why the Nations Rage: Killing in the Name of God*.)

When it comes to the subject of national self-consciousness, and the influences that created it, the debate is endless. A spectacular amount of academic ink has been spilt over it. The mainstream view, as we shall see, is that the nation state began after the Enlightenment of the eighteenth century. As a result, it comes into the post-religious era, and religion's role in creating it is thus played down.

But is this essentially secular view correct? I shall argue here that it is not, and that Christianity played a key role in the development of the nation state. Not only that, but the Reformation itself, with its very different understanding of what makes someone a Christian, was equally crucial.

WHEN DID NATIONALIST CONSCIOUSNESS TRULY BEGIN?

The main consensus among historians, and those of Marxist outlook such as Eric Hobsbawm in particular, is that the nation state is what they call a 'construct of modernity'. In plain English, that means that it is something which arose in modern times and, such writers normally assert, as a result of the overthrow of monarchically based governments, starting with the end of the French *Ancien Régime*. Followers of postmodernism go one stage further and refer to the Age of Modernity lasting two centuries – 1789 to 1989, the French Revolution to the fall of the Berlin Wall and the end of communism in central Europe.

While this has a certain appeal, a growing number of us in the academic community are beginning to question this orthodoxy. While our reasons often differ, many of us are coming to the view that religion played a much more important role in the origins of

national consciousness. Futhermore, we are tending to break the
link between the modern, post-1789 state, and the dawn of the
nation state.

One of the most often cited works in this burgeoning debate
is Liah Greenfeld's *Nationalism: Five Roads to Modernity*. While
she still makes the nation/modernity link, which I reject, it is
nonetheless significant that she puts England as the progenitor of
the modern nation, not post-revolutionary France, and that she
attributes considerable weight to Elizabethan England. In this
she is surely right.

The writers questioning the modernist orthodoxy are in the
main not themselves religious, which makes their contribution all
the more interesting. The best-known protagonist of a different
view is the sociologist Anthony Smith of the London School of
Economics. The author of numerous books on nationalism, he
takes what one might describe as a middle way between the
opposing schools of thought. So let us look at the rivals and see
what Smith and others have to say.

Hitherto, the main opposing school to the modernists have
been the *primordialists*, who say that the nation state is a very
ancient construct, often going back thousands of years. Those
adhering to such a notion are a very mixed group, from the
peaceful to the barbaric.

Among those firmly in the peaceful camp are thinkers such
as the Irish writer Conor Cruise O'Brien. In his essay *The Wrath
of Ages*, he says that there was evident national consciousness in
the Children of Israel, and that as a result such a phenomenon can
be seen as early as the days of the Old Testament.

For Christians, such opinions can ring true. The Jews of the
Old Covenant had a clear sense of self-identity as the chosen
people of God, and a strong attachment to the land that God had
given them. From a theological point of view, though, God's
promises were always tied up with just behaviour and obedience
to his laws. But there can be little doubt that O'Brien is right to
say that there was a real awareness of national self-identity,

however primitive it might appear to us today; and we can also add that it was spiritual as well as political in its nature.

There are also millions of Jews in the world today, and some of them are living in the original Promised Land. Here however the situation is not so simple. The reason that they are there is because a modern country, Britain, gave them the right of safe return in 1917. The overwhelming majority of Jews have not lived in the Holy Land continuously since Old Testament times and indeed not even predominantly in the Middle East.

This is why the defenders of the modernist view reject primordialism: because states which unquestionably existed in ancient times have not existed continuously since then. Not only the Jews suffered the fate of exile. Countless other national or ethnic groupings have been hither and yon in the numerous great migrations of the past two thousand years. In Roman times, whole people groups such as the Magyars (Hungarians) and Slavs of all descriptions lived thousands of miles away from their present-day habitats.

As my Welsh relations remind me, the English did not live in Great Britain until almost four centuries after the birth of Christ. If my wife knew her distant Choctaw relatives, they would tell her that the white man is a very recent addition to the North American continent.

MODERNITY, PRIMORDIALISM AND THEIR MURDEROUS DOWNSIDE

The trouble with the modernist view is that it feels contrary to common sense. We do *not* feel all that new, especially in Europe. This perception could, for example, be part of the slow growing apart between the Old World and the New that has been on the increase since the end of the Cold War, which did so much to bind both sides of the Atlantic together against a common Soviet enemy.

The downside of the primordial view, though, is that it has had some very unpleasant twentieth-century adherents, from the

Nazis through to the genocidal ideologues in Serbia who had so much influence there in the Milošević regime of the 1990s.

But before we go on to look at these two versions of nationalist extremism, we need to look at the compromise theory, or what Professor Smith has described as the gourmet theory of nationalism. This is the way of looking at nationalism which convinces me the most, since it places a proper understanding of history at the centre, gives religion its due importance, but also recognizes that the countries we see in existence today are very different from those that existed in the past.

The negative side of this theory is that you get thoroughly attacked from both sides by the proponents of the other two! Adherence to this middle way therefore requires a certain degree of bravery. Nonetheless, I hope that by the end of this chapter (and the book) you will agree with my way of looking at things. This is because I am coming to the theory from a religious perspective myself, which is not by any means the case with most of those who argue in its favour.

A QUICK LOOK AT THE GOURMET THEORY
OF NATIONALISM

To Professor Anthony Smith and his school of thought, present-day nations are, as a look at any old map will tell you, modern constructions. One only has to see a map made as recently as 1989 to grasp this. The Soviet Union has since vanished, to be replaced by numerous new countries, some of which, like Estonia, existed before 1940, but others, such as Belarus, had never had an independent existence from the USSR. The many European countries listed as People's Republics are no more, and one of them, Czechoslovakia, is now two countries. What was once one Yugoslav state is now five states (and more than that if one counts Kosovo as a separate country and Montenegro as a likely breakaway state). Since 2002 not even the name Yugoslavia itself remains any more.

But if one surveys a map of Europe in the year in which the

late Queen Mother was born, 1900, one sees this even more. There are three enormous empires – Austro-Hungarian, German and Russian, all of which had vanished by 1918. A large country such as Poland appears nowhere, since it had been abolished and carved up by those three empires in the eighteenth century. A state which still exists and existed then, Greece, is there, but much smaller than it is today, and the boundaries of nations such as France and Italy are also different.

In fact one could argue that the Europe we see today is exceptionally new, a product of the end of the Cold War in 1989–91, and thus not much more than a decade old.

However, a common-sense view of the world would seem to point to the fact that while, for example, the present boundary of Germany dates back only to 1990, the German nation is much older. Although no unified German state existed prior to 1871, there has been a kind of German nation and a sense of Germanness for hundreds of years, if not for well over a millennium. The same applies to Italy, which early-nineteenth-century politicians dismissed as a mere 'geographic expression' because in 1800 Italy was split up into a patchwork of many states, a large number of which were under foreign domination.

So this core of what had existed in the past, but did not find precise political demarcation until more recent times, is what Smith calls an *ethnie*.

In other words, Germany as a political entity originated in the late nineteenth century, and during the twentieth century saw its boundaries change considerably as a result of two world wars and the Cold War division of 1949–90. But as an ethnic and cultural grouping, the Germans are a very ancient people, stretching back to before the time of Christ.

What Smith's gourmet theory does is to marry the political modern nature of, say, the German state, with the cultural antiquity of, for example, the German people. In this way, I would argue, he is attuned to present-day realities without defying common sense, as do both the modernists and their primordialist foes. What Smith and I would say is that it is not really possible to have nationalist sentiment without a very old core around which it can be built.

Russia, for example, took a long time to become a unified state, and spent many decades under the alien rule of the Mongol-originated Golden Horde. There is thus no continuity *politically* in the Russian state, and the Russia we have at the moment did not exist before 1991, since between 1917 and 1991 it was subsumed in the Union of Soviet Socialist Republics. But ever since the tenth century, when the diverse Russian peoples converted to the Orthodox Christian faith, there has been a strong sense of Russian ethnic and cultural identity. Religion has consistently played a powerful part in that sense of Russian-ness, even though there has not always been a single independent Russian state.

THE ROLE OF SALVATION RELIGIONS

Perhaps, from the point of view of this book, and I imagine most of its readers, one of the most important of Smith's theories is the critical role played by what he calls *salvation religions.*

As he points out, no one today believes in Jupiter, even though the Roman Empire was one of the most potent in history. The Jewish faith, on the other hand, has survived for thousands of years, and does so successfully today.

Both Christianity and Islam are international, missionary-orientated, multi-ethnic faiths. There are Christians and Muslims of virtually every nation imaginable. This is because these two are faiths based upon salvation, and one does not have to be a member of any particular race, gender or country in order to join. As a consequence, they have symbols that have resonated down the centuries and have proved to be powerful magnets for millions of adherents.

Countries or empires that either adopt or manipulate such symbols can give themselves potent longevity. The Holy Roman Empire, which at one stage stretched from the Danish border in the north to near Naples in the south, managed to last for just over a thousand years. The German word for empire is *Reich*, and the fact that this, the first German-centred empire, lasted for 1006 years – the second German empire for much less, 1871–1918 – was used by Hitler as a symbol of how long his third empire or *Reich* would last.

So we see that the twentieth century demonstrated that salvation religions can also be perverted. The thankfully short-lived Third Reich is a classic example of this, and one that shows what happens when people who have a primordial view of themselves and their country take absolute power.

THE NAZIS AS A CLASSIC EXAMPLE OF BELIEF IN PRIMORDIAL NATIONALISM

The psychoanalyst Carl Jung once said that if one wanted a real understanding of the appeal of Nazism, one only had to look at the cult of the old pagan god Woden (from whom we get the day of the week Wednesday: *Woden's day*). It is possible to see the logic of this when examining the strong emphasis on Nordic mythology in the Third Reich, and the way in which Germany's pagan pre-Christian past received such prominence, especially among the SS. (Jesus being Jewish was clearly an embarrassment.)

But while Hitler himself did not go along with some of the more bizarre occult and racial theories of his lieutenants (satirized in films such as *Indiana Jones* and *Indiana Jones and the Last Crusade*), recent historians have nonetheless shown us that Nazism had a profoundly religious outlook. It can be described as *political religion*, and this is where I part company with Roger Griffin, whose considerably apt and helpful idea of palingenetics we looked at in Chapter 2. Griffin says that palingenetics when applied to fascism is *not* religious, because fascism in its different forms is *this-world* orientated, whereas religion deals with the eternal and transcendent.

However, I rather agree with the expert Professor Michael Burleigh in his book *The Third Reich: A New History*. In that work, he shows that although Hitler always stated that his outlook was scientific, there was nevertheless a strongly pseudo-messianic cult around him that could be seen as profoundly religious. Burleigh calls this religious science, since the kind of racial theories advocated by the Nazis could not be called scientific in any proper sense of the term. Hitler was very much a Christ substitute for a German people traumatized by their defeat in the First World War, and this substitution of the Führer for the Messiah was to get stronger as the Third Reich progressed.

Much of what Hitler was trying to achieve was to resurrect a mythic Germanic past, purified, in his view, from the Jewish and other elements that he saw as contaminating it. (Here we can see the obvious palingenetic application, a myth-based ultra-nationalism.) In finding the kind of Germany that he felt was needed, it was necessary to have a strongly primordial view of German nationalism, a continuum going back to a golden age of a racially pure Germany in the Teutonic forest.

The consequences of such racial nationalism are well known: Jews were slaughtered, as being racially unclean. There is also no question that had Hitler prevailed, he would have sought to eliminate the Church. Tragically, many misguided Christians, especially those in the pro-Nazi German Church, not only failed to oppose Nazism but actually supported it. Bonhoeffer and groups such as the Kreisau Circle among Protestants, and the brave Catholic Bishop of Münster were, alas, a minority. The spiritual cost of the decision of many ordinary Germans to put their patriotism above their faith, and to follow an all too human false messiah rather than the real one, was very high. Hitler despised the churches and, given time, would surely have done even more against them than the occasional imprisonment of brave pastors, like Niemöller, or the harassment of non-compliant local churches by SS thugs.

THE SERBS AS ANOTHER KIND OF MURDEROUS PRIMORDIALIST

Many in Europe thought that the genocidal mania of the middle part of the last century was long since behind us. Events in the

1990s, with which we began this chapter, revealed that this view was a sad delusion, and few events more than the mass murder of Bosnian Muslims by Serb forces in the wars that followed the break-up of the old Yugoslavia.

Here one must be fair and say that the Bosnian Muslims themselves were not entirely guiltless. And some of the hideous massacres, such as the one at Ahmici, made famous to British television viewers by its discovery by Colonel Bob Stewart and the Cheshire Regiment, were carried out by Croat irregular soldiers. But American personnel I met who had served in the region, along with official sources in the USA, did not hesitate to ascribe at least 80 per cent of the killing to Serb troops, whether official soldiers or irregular gangs, such as those led by the infamous Serb warlord, Arkan.

The Serb nationalist sentiment that gave rise to such carnage dates back to the era in between the death of the Yugoslav national hero and dictator, Marshal Tito, and the eruption into civil war just over ten years later. Tito was half-Slovene and half-Croat, and thus not a full member of any of the different nationalities that made up the Yugoslav federation. He was also the one central European ruler who, in the Second World War, was able to liberate his own country from German and Italian occupation, and was thus able to survive Soviet attempts to depose him in the 1940s and impose a puppet ruler.

After Tito died, the glue with which he had been able to hold the country together began to become unstuck. Many of the nationalities began to look to their own interests and, in the case of the smaller groups, such as the Croatians, Slovenes and Bosnian Muslims, began to fear what the larger Serb population would do. In return, the Serbs started to fear for the Serb minorities in the other parts of the Federation, especially if the country were to break up.

During this transitional phase in the 1980s, the Serb Academy of Sciences propounded what was called a Greater Serbia thesis. They argued that if the federal Yugoslav state collapsed, then Serbia, its largest component, should reclaim the territory that had belonged to the Serb kingdom at its peak in the Middle Ages. Here again we see palingenetics at work, with a strongly religious component.

LONGING FOR A LOST MEDIEVAL EMPIRE AND ITS TERRIBLE TWENTIETH-CENTURY CONSEQUENCES

The Serbian nationalists who congregated around Slobodan Milošević and others looked back with longing to a medieval Serb empire which, for a brief time, stretched as far down as the Aegean and was one of the most powerful states in the Balkans. In particular, Serbs look back to the reign of Emperor Stephan Dušan, who reigned over Serbia from 1331 to 1355, and who in 1345 gave himself the title of Emperor of the Serbs and the Greeks. But only thirty-four years after Dušan's death, the Serb Empire, which was already in a state of advanced disintegration, received a mortal wound. This was the battle of Kosovo Polje, the Field of Blackbirds. This conflict has gone down in Serb legend, which is strange because it was a battle that the Serbs *lost*. (It is rather as if the French annually celebrated the battle of Waterloo.) The Serb prince, Lazar, was killed, as was the Turkish leader. In reality, Serbs fought on both sides of the battle, and the actual outcome was an effective draw, since the rump Serbian realm was not conquered until the following century.

However, the Serbs had to suffer five centuries of Ottoman oppression – as did all the other many conquered Balkan peoples, such as the Greeks, Bulgarians and Romanians. The Ottoman Turks went on to conquer most of Hungary in 1526, and almost succeeded in capturing Austria. It was not until the 1680s that the West Europeans were able to begin to turn the tide and start the very slow process of liberating the Balkan peninsula. The southern part of Greece won independence in the 1830s, and Serbia began to regain self-rule in the 1850s. But it was not until just before the First World War that Ottoman rule over the region was finally curtailed.

This was very hard for all the Balkan peoples. I put it like this because, although Bosnian Muslims, Croats and Serbs have killed each other or been killed in abundance, they are *ethnically* exactly the same. It is their history and their religion that differentiates Orthodox Serbs, Catholic Croats and Muslim Bosnians one from the other. Until the 1990s they were regarded as speaking the same language as well, which they now deny.

KILLING THE TURKS IN THE NAME OF GOD

The Serbs resented the rule of people who were not just aliens, but of a different religion as well – Islam. For them the situation was also worsened in that many Slavs living in present-day Bosnia converted, many voluntarily, to the Muslim faith. These converts – today's Bosnian Muslims, or Bosniaks – were regarded as traitors by their Serb neighbours. Soon, they started to think of them not as fellow Slavs but as 'Turks', people of the same ethnic origin as their Ottoman oppressors. Genetically and historically this was pure nonsense, but this belief was eventually to have a deadly result.

Over the course of time, and especially by the era of the struggle for independence in the late eighteenth and nineteenth centuries, a whole series of myths about the battle of Kosovo had grown up. The Serbs saw themselves increasingly in spiritual terms, as a suffering people. They saw Lazar as a Christ figure, who gave his life for his people. The myth of Heavenly Serbia arose and became virtually official ideology after the 1850s, when Serbia began its path to independence.

A POEM BY A BISHOP PRAISES MASS MURDERERS

One of the most famous poems of Slavic literature is the nineteenth-century epic *The Mountain Wreath*. The author was the Montenegrin Bishop Peter II Njegoš. (The Montenegrins are ethnic Serbs who managed to get independence earlier than their fellow Serbs over in Serbia.)

It is, as a recent British writer has put it, a paean to genocide, mass murder and ethnic cleansing. It is an account of the massacre of local Slavic Muslims by a gang of Serb rebels, instigated by no less than a bishop, and done explicitly in the name of Christ. Once again, the victims were called 'Turks' or 'Turkifiers', and the murderers saw themselves as doing a holy deed.

It would seem extraordinary to us that people could commit such atrocities for Christian reasons. Even worse, one could argue that it began a chain of slaughter and counter-slaughter that has continued up to the present. Thousands of people have been butchered at regular intervals – in the 1870s, before and during the First World War, again in the Second World War and then once more in the 1990s, right up to the massacres of innocent Kosovar Albanians by the Serbs in 1999.

The young man with whom we began this chapter shows that the sentiments of late-twentieth-century Serb killers was no different from those of their ancestors at the end of the eighteenth. To him, his victims were 'Turks', even though they were ethnically and linguistically exactly the same as he was. Somehow, calling them by another name made it all right to kill them, especially since Bosnian Muslims and Bosnian Serbs had often grown up together in the same town or village, going to school together, working together and much else besides.

Their warped logic was that because Ottoman Turks ruled the Balkans for five centuries, and committed atrocities against the local population, then it was quite all right to murder those of your neighbours who have not oppressed anyone but shared the religion of the hated but now departed conqueror.

SEEING OUR NEIGHBOURS AS A PLAGUE
INSTEAD OF LOVING THEM

That rationale behind all such gruesome behaviour, including that of the mass rapes of Bosnian Muslim women by Serb soldiers in the 1990s, is very similar to the Nazi thinking behind the genocide of the Jews in the 1940s. It is that people different from us are a kind of plague to be got rid of so that we can have an ethnically pure state, where no one who is unlike us will live.

What made the Serb atrocities worse, from the point of view of this book, is that it was often done in the name of a pure Orthodox Serbia, uncontaminated by the pollution of Muslims. While some Serb Orthodox leaders were horrified at the slaughter, others, while never directly condoning it, were not at all displeased with the results: a great increase in Serb-ruled territory and the removal of Muslims from cities where they had lived alongside Serbs for decades.

(The Orthodox Serbs were not alone in their recourse to murder. Many Catholic Croats committed equal acts of savagery during the fighting, in the same way that their pro-Nazi parents and grandparents had done in the 1940s. They carried out their own version of ethnic cleansing, especially in 1995 when Croatian forces were able to counter-attack. One of the encouraging pieces of news from this area is in the Bosnian town of Mostar. Protestant Croats, who are neither Catholic Croat nor Bosnian Muslim, established a charity called *Novimost*, which has been active in getting children from both sides of the conflict together. It is a small operation but at least it is an active start in the right direction.)

This is not in any way to belittle Nazi atrocities – and in the 1940s, it was often the Serbs who were the victims of genocidal murder either by German occupation forces or their local allies, the *Ustasa*. It is just that the motivation was different – racial in the case of the Nazis, and religious nationalist in the case of the Serbs in the 1990s.

This too we can see easily in the light of palingenetic theory. The myth is that of Heavenly Serbia, of Lazar the Christ figure and substitute, and of the present-day Serbs as those taking holy revenge for the bad deeds done to their ancestors. So I would argue that the myth-based ultra-nationalism of Serbia is strongly religious in tone and motivation, even though those who exploited such feelings, like Slobodan Milošević, were themselves far from religious.

SO WHEN DID NATIONALISM BEGIN AND
DID RELIGION PLAY A ROLE IN ITS BIRTH?

There is a strong argument for national identity beginning far earlier than the current orthodoxy supposes. Some, like the Catholic historian, Adrian Hastings, have put it as early as the Middle Ages, and made England the starting point. While such a date has more credibility than that of the French Revolution, I think that is starting too early. Even England could not really be said to have a full *national* sense of identity in what was still a feudal era, where your main allegiance was to your local lord, and your conception of life beyond your local town or village was somewhat limited.

In addition, until the fifteenth century, as historians such as Norman Davies have shown, the English Kings themselves were, until King Henry IV and the Lancastrian dynasty, more French than they were English. Not until the end of the fourteenth century do we get English Kings speaking the language of their own people, and it was not really until the time of Chaucer that we saw the beginnings of a nationally accepted way of speaking the English language.

I think that the Reformation is a much more likely time to start thinking about the origins of what we would now call *national* as opposed to purely local self-consciousness. We will now examine this idea.

WHY THE REFORMATION AND THE INVENTION OF
PRINTING ARE A BETTER STARTING POINT

What is significant about the early sixteenth century, and the dawn of the Protestant Reformation, as a true starting point is that historians who support other beginning dates themselves agree on its considerable importance. One of those who did so was Adrian Hastings, in his work *The Construction of Nationhood: Ethnicity, Religion and Nationalism*. (Note the due importance he gave to religion in the subtitle.) He rightly gave very considerable weight to a key part of the Reformation – the translation of the Bible into the vernacular. All those who were literate could now read the Bible in their own language.

That is not to say that educated people had not been able to read it before: the survival of many lectionaries and Books of Hours, in Latin, from the later Middle Ages shows that lay people as well as clergy were reading the word of God. But they had to do so in an alien language. With the coming of the Reformation, with translations such as those of Tyndale, Coverdale (and later on the Geneva Bible), this extra step ceased to be necessary. Anyone who read their own language could now read Scripture along with everything else available.

This meant that literate people up and down the country were now able to read the *same* book, not to mention any amount of Protestant pamphlets, commentaries, devotional literature and much else besides. It meant that each local language was further homogenized in a way that was more difficult hitherto, printers now having to choose between regional variations and dialects and create a standard version of the language.

The other great transformation was technical – a scientific discovery that was to have the profoundest of *spiritual* results. This was the invention of the printing press by Gutenberg in the fifteenth century, his famous printed Bible appearing in 1455.

This was to have a revolutionary impact. No longer was it necessary to copy out manuscripts laboriously by hand – one team of people could produce hundreds, if not thousands, of exact copies by the new invention. This also meant that ideas could be spread much more rapidly. Readers the length of Europe could pick up and consider the same ideas. Debate could take place on a scale hitherto impossible. Since pictures (woodcuts) could also be printed, even semi-literate or illiterate lay people could see what was being discussed and join in for themselves.

This had the result that soon after Martin Luther had nailed his famous 95 theses on reforming the Church to the door of the church in Wittenberg, what began as a local debate was soon being argued over across Europe. Pamphlets by Luther, and for and against his teaching, were soon being sold and distributed in their thousands.

One of Luther's cardinal tenets concerned the abolition of a separate priestly caste, and the rediscovery of what the Apostle Peter calls, in his Epistle, the *priesthood of all believers*. No longer did you have to believe that only the Church was necessary to mediate between individuals and God: you could have a direct relationship with God yourself. Salvation was by faith alone: *sola fidei* in Latin. Scripture also now proved to be far more important, since you did not need a priest to tell you what it meant. Scripture, not the Church and its interpretation, became the authority on what to believe: *sola scriptura*, 'by scripture alone'.

As a result, Luther translated the Bible into German. As with the English translations, the fact that so many people across a large region were reading the same book and in their own language meant they no longer had to depend on a priest who officiated in Latin and used a Latin Bible. This created a German consciousness that had not existed before.

The other important factor was that the Reformation in places such as Germany and Switzerland was from the bottom up, rather than top down as in England. While it helped that the Elector of Saxony was able to protect Luther from being martyred, the initiative had come from an ordinary monk and was supported strongly by peasants, tradesmen, knights and all kinds of other laity.

Furthermore, the Holy Roman Empire (now effectively reduced to present-day Germany, the Low Countries, Bohemia and Austria) had in it many cities that were not under the control of a local duke or prince, but which owed direct allegiance to the Emperor. It was the same in Switzerland, where the Cantons, such as Zurich and Geneva, were under effectively democratic control. Here it was the decision of the local city council whom to support, and many of the Imperial Free Cities became Protestant by vote rather than by royal decree.

For many such city councillors, in both Switzerland and the Empire, the Reformation, with its abolition of priestly control, was profoundly liberating. One of the factors that persuaded them, and those princes who also backed Luther, was that he was a German and that they too were Germans. No longer would they be under the spiritual authority of someone miles away in Rome, the Pope, or of the Holy Roman Emperor, Charles V, who although he was their nominal sovereign was also King of Spain and ruler of much of Latin America and of large parts of Italy.

In other words, the Reformation played a key role in creating a sense of German unity among its supporters, even though *politically* Germany was a massive patchwork of hundreds of little states, such as the tiny Duchy of Coburg from which the British royal family descends. There was no *single* German state until 1870, and the Holy Roman Empire contained regions that were Czech or Flemish as well as German. But the Holy Roman Empire split into Protestant and Catholic camps (and the Protestant part soon into Lutheran and Calvinist wings), never again to be reunited.

So how does all this apply to us in English-speaking countries such as the United Kingdom, Canada and the United States? Just because we have not had mass murder on the scale of the former Yugoslavia (besides which Northern Ireland pales in comparison) or a racist genocidal maniac like Hitler as our political leader, that does not mean that we are exempt from criticism. We too have our myths and they have been profoundly influenced by our Christian history. That will be the theme of the next chapter.

4

The Tower of Babel

Where did the exclusive kind of nationalism that we saw in the last chapter begin? This chapter and the next will look at biblical teaching on who God's people are. We will then go on, in later chapters, to see how Christians have interpreted this issue in their own countries at different times, right up until the present. The word *genesis* means 'beginning' and I will therefore begin there in looking at the Bible's view of who we are and how we relate to other people. The issue of inclusive and exclusive identity – the theme of the last chapter – is very ancient, and goes back as far as when people first started to form themselves into social groups. One of the key teachings of Scripture is that human nature always remains the same.

One of the most memorable scenes in the Old Testament is the Tower of Babel, immortalized in the famous Bruegel picture. Quotations from the book of Genesis can open an exegetical can of worms, depending upon your view of Scripture. However, in the case of Babel, I think that either a literal or a metaphorical reading of the passage can lead us to the same conclusion. On that basis, we can examine the story, and that of Abraham that follows after it.

Babel can be described as the beginning of linguistic diversity. It has been used as a defence of separate nationhood. God created the differing people groups that resulted from the Babel diaspora. But what is the reason given for God's decision? It was their *sin*. They wanted to build a tower that would reach to the heavens, and communicate with God in a way of their choosing, rather than his. As Francis Schaeffer puts it, when the people decided to make a name for *themselves* they were in effect making

The first public declaration of humanism ... The Bible indicates here, as it does constantly in the early chapters of Genesis, that all the divisions of the whole world are a result of sin and the righteous judgement of God. (*Genesis in Space and Time* (1972), pp. 152–3)

Schaeffer has defined humanism (in its twentieth-century sense) as independence from God. In that sense, Babel is exactly that – man's declaration of self-rule. It is, as Derek Kidner observed, 'timelessly characteristic of the spirit of the world [and] the motto of modern nationalism' (*Genesis* (1967), pp. 109–10).

PUNISHMENT OR BLESSING?

A fundamental characteristic of humankind is the ability to communicate thoughts. Thus the resulting separation of people groups after Babel frustrates the innermost desire of people to communicate with one another. Genesis tells us that God has separated nations one from another as a sign of judgement upon the arrogance shown at Babel. Linguistic differences, thus, are a means of humbling the proud, not a matter of pride or celebration. Separation of languages leads to separation of nations.

Separate nationhood is thus a curse, not a blessing. It results from our failure to behave responsibly when trusted by God. So it is odd that some Christian commentators, such as the late Raymond Johnston, have seen Babel in a different light. To them, God is establishing linguistic and cultural diversity, and therefore the different national and language distinctions that now exist are a good thing.

Many of my Welsh relatives joke that they will not have to learn a new language when they get to heaven because they speak its language already! But humour apart, it does seem strange that we regard something that happens as a result of sin and rebellion against God as being good. God is deliberately *disuniting* us in order to keep us apart and punish us, so that we will not unite against him in rebellion again.

GOD CHOOSES A PEOPLE FOR HIMSELF

Following Babel, God, after many generations, chooses a people for himself. He picks out Abraham and starts what we now know as the Jewish race. Even here, though, we see that it is in effect a temporary expedient. We see in Genesis 12.3 that 'all peoples on earth will be blessed through you'. The new nation was specific, but the ultimate blessing would be international.

This is reinforced in Genesis 18.17–19:

> Then the LORD said, 'Shall I hide from Abraham what I am about to do? Abraham will surely become a great and powerful nation, and all nations on earth will be blessed through him. For I have chosen him, so that he will direct his children and his household after him to keep the way of the LORD by doing what is right and just, so that the LORD will bring about for Abraham what he has promised him.'

One can interpret this passage by saying that as God created a nation, therefore nations as such are all right. God, having instituted the existence of nations as discrete entities at Babel, now creates one of his own. But I think that another kind of interpretation is better.

ALL NATIONS ARE TO BE BLESSED
THROUGH ABRAHAM

First, it is clear that *all* the nations will be blessed through Abraham. God's blessing is not nation-specific. This is now understood as a prophecy of Christ himself, Abraham's descendant. But it shows that even at this early date, God's plans included the whole of humanity in their scope. It is not the glorification of *nationhood*, nor is it the elevation of one nation above others. Rather it is God using one nation to bless all of them, in what will turn out to be a multinational plan of salvation.

Second, all depends on whether or not the family and household follow God. Merely to be a part of the Jewish nation is never enough. Here the Bible is markedly different from nationalist movements, for whom accident of birth is everything. You can have the right ancestry and *not* be chosen.

We see this first with Abraham's own descendants. Ishmael is sent away (Genesis 21) and Esau, even though he is senior in birth, is not chosen over Jacob (Genesis 25 and 27). Much of the nationalism of the twentieth century has been based upon *jus sanguinis*, the law of blood descent. In such terms, Ishmael and Esau have equal rights of descent.

HOW PAUL INTERPRETS THE OLD TESTAMENT

This is something clarified theologically by the Apostle Paul in his Epistle to the Romans. Paul was himself *ethnically* Jewish, but was now a Christian by persuasion. As he shows in his autobiographical writings, no one was originally more proud of his ancestry than he. But he came to understand that the Christian faith into which he had come was very different. He told the Christians in Rome, who were of both Jewish and non-Jewish descent, that

> not all who are descended from Israel are Israel. Nor because they are his descendants are they all Abraham's children. On the contrary, 'It is through Isaac that your offspring will be reckoned.' In other words, it is not the natural children who are God's children, but it is the children of the promise who are regarded as Abraham's offspring. (Romans 9.6–8)

This was not something that should have come as a surprise to Paul's readers, especially those familiar with the Old Testament.

AMOS AND THE PEOPLE OF GOD

We can also see this in the writing of the prophet Amos, who lived towards the end of the Israelite northern kingdom. Even though they had the right ancestry and outwardly worshipped God, their apostasy and their oppressive behaviour would cause their doom:

> I hate, I despise your religious feasts;
>> I cannot stand your assemblies.
> Even though you bring me burnt offerings and grain
>> offerings,
>> I will not accept them.
>
>   (Amos 5.21–2)

Not only that, but God no longer saw them as any different from the other nations around them:

> 'Are not you Israelites
>> the same to me as Cushites?'
>> declares the LORD.

> 'Did I not bring Israel up from Egypt,
>> the Philistines from Caphtor
>> and the Arameans from Kir?

> Surely the eyes of the Sovereign LORD
>> are on the sinful kingdom.
> I will destroy it
>> from the face of the earth.
>
>   (Amos 9.7–8)

Soon the Kingdom of Israel was no more. Yet the position was not hopeless, for God promised to 'restore David's fallen tent' (Amos 9.11). When we read the accounts of Ezra and of Nehemiah, we know that some of God's people were able to return to the land of their ancestors.

GOD'S TRUE KINGDOM

God's relationship with his people, therefore, was with those who believed in him and followed his commandments. Oppressors of the poor, worshippers of other gods, whoever they might be genetically, were not a part of the true kingdom of God.

Israel, then, was not simply a nation in the geographical, historical or biological sense of the word that we understand by 'nation' today. It was a people chosen by God for *spiritual* ends. Those who rejected that spiritual calling, from the king downwards, were not part of God's Israel, however much they might be part of the political, geographical, ethnic unit called by that name.

As the story of Naaman the Syrian tells us, you could belong to God and be outside the physical boundaries of the kingdom. In Isaiah we see God describing even a non-believer such as Cyrus as an instrument of divine will. The book of Esther demonstrates that God could be with you in exile as well as in the Promised Land. God's people were no longer geographically based.

The prophet Ezekiel foresaw a day when the aliens living in the territory of the Israelites would have the same rights to live there as the Children of Israel themselves.

JESUS THE FULFILMENT OF OLD TESTAMENT PROPHECY

This certainly came to pass in a spiritual sense when Jesus, the long-awaited Messiah, was born. The passage in Isaiah 9, 'to us a child is born', is often read at Christmas. But we often forget the opening part:

> In the past he humbled the land of Zebulun and the land of Naphtali, but in the future he will honour Galilee of the Gentiles [or *nations* in the RSV]. (Isaiah 9.1)

We also forget that the passage which comes after that messianic prophecy gives a dire warning of severe judgement by God against the people of Israel:

> But the people have not returned to him who has struck them,
>   nor have they sought the LORD Almighty.
> So the Lord will cut off from Israel both head and tail,
>   both palm branch and reed in a single day.
>   (Isaiah 9.13–14)

Help for those who turn to God is at hand. But the context of it, again in a messianic prophetic passage, is interesting.

> I, the LORD, have called you in righteousness;
>   I will take hold of your hand.
> I will keep you and will make you
>   to be a covenant for the people
>   and a light for the Gentiles [RSV: *nations*],
> to open eyes that are blind,
>   to free captives from prison
>   and to release from the dungeon those who sit in
>   darkness.
>
> (Isaiah 42.6–7)

About his servant, the saviour of Israel, God says:

> It is too small a thing for you to be my servant
>   to restore the tribes of Jacob
>   and bring back those of Israel I have kept.
> I will also make you a light for the Gentiles,
>   that you may bring my salvation to the ends of the
>   earth . . .
> See, I will beckon to the Gentiles,
>   I will lift up my banner to the peoples;
> they will bring your sons in their arms,
>   and carry your daughters on their shoulders.
>
> (Isaiah 49.6, 22)

It is therefore in fulfilment of what the author of Isaiah foretold that when Jesus is presented as a child in the Temple, Simeon says:

> Sovereign Lord, as you have promised,
> you now dismiss your servant in peace.
> For my eyes have seen your salvation,
> which you have prepared in the sight of all people,
> a light for revelation to the Gentiles [also *Gentiles* in RSV]
> and for glory to your people Israel.
>
> (Luke 2.29–32)

Salvation will no longer be either ethnically based or geographically centred. The coming of Jesus represents God choosing a people for himself not any longer mainly around a nation, but of faithful people from all nations. As Jesus told the Samaritan woman at the well,

> Believe me, woman, a time is coming when you will worship the Father neither on this mountain [where the Samaritans did] nor in Jerusalem [where the Jews did]. You Samaritans worship what you do not know; we worship what we do know, for salvation is from the Jews. Yet a time is coming and has now come when the true worshippers will worship the Father in spirit and in truth, for they are the kind of worshippers the Father seeks. God is spirit, and his worshippers must worship in spirit and in truth. (John 4.21–4)

JESUS THE MESSIAH FOR ALL THE WORLD

It is surely significant that Christ proclaims his messianic status to someone who is a woman, since men had to be very circumspect in talking to women outside their family. She was also of low moral repute: why else was she out alone at noon in the heat of the midday sun? She was also a Samaritan, a member of a race that had interbred with the local inhabitants and who also failed to worship God in the prescribed way. She was therefore unsuitable by gender, morals and ethnicity. Yet she is the person to whom Jesus says, in response to her comment that the Messiah is coming, 'I who speak to you am he' (verse 26).

Later, at the end of his ministry, when Jesus is about to ascend back into heaven, he tells the disciples that they

> will receive power when the Holy Spirit comes on you; and you will be my witnesses in Jerusalem, and in all Judea and Samaria, and to the ends of the earth. (Acts 1.8)

Then, at Pentecost, people from all over the Roman part of the world do come to Jerusalem, and are converted. All these people would either have been Jews or proselytes, but they would be taking the Christian message to cultures and places well beyond the confines of Palestine.

THE CHRISTIAN CHURCH SPREADS TO
GENTILES LIKE US

For the minority of us raised in Christian homes, the downside about learning so much of the Bible when we are children is that we continue to think of many passages in a childlike way. We fail to think through the full implications. A good example of the spread of the gospel is the story of Philip and the Ethiopian eunuch in Acts 8.

Eunuchs were forbidden in Deuteronomy 23 from taking full part in Jewish ritual and worship. This eunuch would therefore also have been excluded. Despite this, the narrative tells us that he had nonetheless travelled the huge distance from his part of Africa to go to Jerusalem to worship. In addition, since he was reading the Book of Isaiah in his chariot, he was clearly very well aware of Jewish beliefs, even if he did not understand their full meaning.

His conversion and baptism into the Christian Church is therefore one of double meaning. A group hitherto banned now became fully eligible since his emasculated status was no bar to becoming a Christian. He was also someone entirely non-Jewish, and is thus one of the most prominent of the early Gentile converts to the new faith. Truly Christianity is universal, and is neither ethnically nor geographically specific.

A little later in the Book of Acts we see the conversion of the Roman centurion Cornelius. Here again the nature of the new Christian is interesting – a member of the hated imperial army of occupation, someone no self-respecting Jewish nationalist would ever contemplate meeting. It is as if a German officer were to be converted in, say, Poland during the Second World War. (Cornelius hitherto had the status of 'god-fearer', someone not a full proselyte but who observed Jewish ritual and custom.)

Peter's instinctive reaction was probably like one that a loyal Polish partisan would have had. However, the vision that he had from God, that of ritually unclean meat which God commanded him to eat, showed him that he had to abandon his prejudices. As Peter describes it:

> You are well aware that it is against our law for a Jew to associate with a Gentile or visit him. But God has shown me that I should not call any man impure or unclean. So when I was sent for, I came [to the home of Cornelius] without raising any objection. (Acts 10.28–9)

Once again, many of us would be familiar with this story from childhood and Sunday School. We will probably remember the main point: that Peter realized that Gentiles, like us, can now be full members of the Church. Christianity is not only for former Jews like Peter. But we fail, alas, to see the radical nature of the message that is being proclaimed. We need to think about such passages in a mature adult way for the full force of the message to strike us correctly.

CHRISTIAN FAITH AND RACIAL PREJUDICE

I think that there are wider implications in terms of what we are discussing in this book. What does it tell us, for example, about racial prejudice? One of the interesting things about a multiracial society is that those of different skin colour or culture are no longer 'over there', thousands of miles away, but right here, in our own society, next door. Jews had every reason politically to dislike the Romans, who had deprived them of political independence. They were normally (people such as Cornelius excepted) pagans with barbaric practices, such as putting people horribly to death in the circus for fun, and oppressive rulers who imposed harsh and possibly unjust taxes on their unwilling subjects.

Yet now the infant Church has within it a black Ethiopian eunuch and a Roman centurion. Neither of these could be described as being in categories high on the list of groups to evangelize by choice, but there they were.

In the 1960s, in the USA, some missionary societies realized two things. Firstly, they were keeping the missions under expatriate white control, rather than devolving power to the indigenous Christians whose countries were now being given political freedom by their European colonial masters. This, the missionaries realized, was quite wrong. It was not simply that if African peoples could run their own country they could certainly run their own churches, though that was true. It was also evident that the white missionaries had been unintentionally racist, not seeing the African Christians as their fully equal brothers and sisters in Christ.

SEEING MISSION AS BEING SOMETHING HERE AT HOME

In addition, they had always seen black people as 'over there', thousands of miles across the Atlantic Ocean. They had failed to see the millions of black Americans in their own country, whose presence in the USA was a result of sin by the missionaries' own white ancestors. It had become all to easy to be a missionary doing good in foreign parts, while ignoring the African neighbours next door. As a result, some missionary societies started to work with African-American churches in evangelism and social concern.

The same has happened in Britain with missionary societies such as Interserve now actively involved with outreach to Asians living in Britain. This, though, is more controversial, since increasing numbers of people in a secular society regard religion as being intrinsically ethnic, and disapprove of interracial proselytization. (Most Afro-Caribbean Britons come from families that are at least nominally Christian, so cross-cultural evangelism is less problematic.) This is highly ironic, since Islam is the one major international faith as deliberately multiracial as Christianity. Hinduism is not, however, though one could describe some New Age followers as being Hindu in some senses of the term. Fortunately much of the evangelism is being done increasingly by

Asian Christians, who are not therefore sharing the gospel across ethnic barriers.

We will be looking at some of these issues in the next chapter, when discussing the matter of how we treat aliens in our own society. Here we need to remember that we too, like Peter and other early Christians, have our prejudices that we need to overcome. One of my former students, an African-American, bemoaned the fact that in much of the USA Sunday is often the most segregated day of the week. Within the context of American history, there are reasons why this is so, but surely, since they originate in the sin of slavery and racial oppression, they are reasons whose effects we should do all we can to overcome?

It is also true that much African-American and Afro-Caribbean worship is quite exuberant, and that people who are used to such an atmosphere might find the more physically restrained nature of white Western worship slightly boring. On the other hand, some Pentecostal and House Church denominations, and charismatic groups within mainstream churches, have the kind of highly emotional style in which white and African can feel fully and equally at home. Likewise, it is pure racial stereotyping to say that all those of African ancestry like extrovert worship. Many theologically more conservative Christians of African-American and Afro-Caribbean descent happily attend churches that many white people consider tame, but which they like because of factors such as a strong emphasis on expository preaching or a more introvert meditative style of liturgy.

The main thing, then, is to do all possible, whether within the walls of one church, or as a unified body of Christians in one town or neighbourhood, to show the world outside that Christ is not divided by colour, ethnicity, gender or any of the many causes that produce so much division and hatred in secular society.

5

Strangers in Our Midst: The Bible and Other Races

In the last chapter, we saw how Christianity is a truly international, transcultural faith. Most of us now live in multicultural societies, for example in a Britain that has long since ceased to be exclusively white or in a United States that, in theory, proclaims itself openly to be a melting-pot country. The ongoing nature of racial tension shows us, alas, that many of our fellow citizens find this a very difficult concept. How, though, should we as Christians react? If a scarlet woman like the Samaritan at the well, or a castrated black African such as the Ethiopian eunuch, are equally welcome into the kingdom of God, in what way should the Church behave to those people who are racially or otherwise different from the majority?

If one looks at the teaching of Scripture, one can see that Christians who treat people ill because they are somehow different from them are acting against what the Bible lays down as the right way to behave.

Israel, in Old Testament times, was filled with people religiously and ethnically distinct from the Jewish majority. The Bible distinguishes between people temporarily visiting and those of different race/faith who are settled permanently in the country. The issue today – of, for example, Muslims of North African or South Asian descent living in France or Britain – is therefore not new. Furthermore, when slaves in Egypt, the children of Israel were themselves strangers or aliens in a foreign land. This means that they should treat similar sojourners in the Promised Land in that light.

We all know that we are commanded to love our neighbour as ourselves. This in itself should act to prevent hostility and prejudice against those different from us. But because we are fallen, God needs to spell it out more specifically for us, and that is what he does in the books of the Pentateuch.

Exodus makes this clear again and again:

> Do not ill-treat an alien or oppress him, for you were aliens in Egypt . . . Do not oppress an alien; you yourselves know how it feels to be aliens, because you were aliens in Egypt. (Exodus 22.21 and 23.9)

So too do other books which follow:

> When an alien lives with you in your land, do not ill-treat him. The alien living with you must be treated as one of your native-born. Love him as yourself, for you were aliens in Egypt. I am the LORD your God. (Leviticus 19.33–4)

> He [God] defends the cause of the fatherless and the widow, and loves the alien, giving him food and clothing. And you are to love those who are aliens, for you yourselves were aliens in Egypt. (Deuteronomy 10.18–19)

Here we see that the alien, dwelling in the Promised Land, has fully the same rights as a child of Israel. To oppress them is no different from ill-treating the fatherless and widows, or from shedding innocent blood (Jeremiah 7.6). When the people of Israel are exiled, God includes the aliens in the newly restored land, as fully equal inhabitants:

> 'You are to allot it as an inheritance for yourselves and for the aliens who have settled among you and who have children. You are to consider them as native-born Israelites; along with you they are to be allotted an inheritance among the tribes of Israel. In whatever tribe the alien settles, there you are to give him his inheritance,' declares the Sovereign LORD. (Ezekiel 47.22–3)

The books of Leviticus and Deuteronomy required the Children of Israel to leave the gleanings of their fields so that the alien could have enough to eat. The alien and the indigenous Jewish poor were seen as one and the same in terms of rights.

As the whole story of the Book of Ruth tells us, there were those who obeyed the command. Furthermore, the great King David, and therefore the entire royal line of Judah, descended from the marriage of Ruth the alien with Boaz the righteous Jew. We know from the New Testament that our Lord himself was of this lineage.

Such a declaration speaks to us in many ways today, regardless of our eschatology. For those for whom the prophecies of the restoration of the land of Israel is *physical*, it surely speaks of the need for the Jewish and Palestinian inhabitants of twenty-first-century Israel to live harmoniously together, and not in permanent conflict, as at present.

For those for whom this passage speaks of an ongoing *spiritual* injunction, the message is equally plain: people different from you, ethnically and religiously, have the right to live at peace with you in the land you inhabit. From a Canaanite pagan then, to a Pakistani Muslim immigrant today, our relationship with neighbours not of our own kind must be informed by biblical love rather than by racial hate and prejudice.

THE NEW TESTAMENT AND LOVING
OUR NEIGHBOUR

Those who returned from exile were not, then, instructed to cleanse the land of the alien, but to live with them on terms of equal treatment and good neighbourliness. Can we, as Christians today, therefore talk disparagingly of immigrants, of being 'swamped', or of restoring 'English' or 'Anglo-Saxon' values? Biblically I think that the answer must be no.

When we come on to the New Testament, the distinction evaporates. Christianity is not a faith just for the Jews, but for believers of all racial backgrounds. The Apostle Paul puts this in several different ways, each one with a special emphasis.

In the Christian Church, there is 'no Greek or Jew, circumcised or uncircumcised, barbarian, Scythian, slave or free, but Christ is all, and is in all' (Colossians 3.11).

> There is neither Jew nor Greek, slave nor free, male nor female, for you are all one in Christ Jesus. If you belong to Christ, then you are Abraham's seed, and heirs according to the promise. (Galatians 3.28–9)

From this we see that there can be no racial, social or gender divisions within the Church. Your ethnicity, gender and socio-economic status outside of the Church make no difference within it. One of the most humbling things for contemporary white Christians in the West is that the overwhelming growth of Christianity is in places such as Africa, Latin America and the Far East. In Britain the bishop of one of the oldest dioceses is of Pakistani birth, and that of one of Britain's largest dioceses is a former Ugandan judge. As the West becomes increasingly secular, or post-Christian as the phenomenon has been called, countries such as Nigeria, where white Europeans went as missionaries in the nineteenth century, are sending missionaries to convert pagan Britain in the twenty-first. Such people, along with the often spiritually vibrant Afro-Caribbean community, are immigrants for whom we should thank God!

Furthermore, the Apostle Paul tells that in fact we as Christians are now ourselves aliens in a non-Christian world. We are not what we once were. Paul therefore wrote as follows to the Gentile converts to Christian faith now in Ephesus:

> As for you, you were dead in your transgressions and sins, in which you used to live when you followed the ways of this world . . . remember that formerly you who are Gentiles by birth . . . that at that time you were separate from Christ, excluded from citizenship in Israel and foreigners to the covenants of the promise, without hope and without God in the world. But now in Christ Jesus you who were once far away have been brought near by the blood of Christ.
>
> For he himself is our peace, who has made the two one

and has destroyed the barrier, the dividing wall of hostility, by abolishing in his flesh the law with its commandments and regulations. His purpose was to create in himself one new man out of the two, thus making peace, and in this one body to reconcile both of them to God through the cross...

Consequently you are no longer foreigners and aliens, but fellow-citizens with God's people and members of God's household, built on the foundation of the apostles and prophets, with Christ Jesus himself as the chief cornerstone. (Ephesians 2.1–2, 11–16 and 19–20).

In other words, Christ has overcome all barriers that hitherto separated Jew and Gentile. All who follow Christ are full and equal members of the household of God.

WE ARE THE BENEFICIARIES OF
BIBLICAL THINKING

Two thousand years after these words were written, Western Christians all too easily forget their importance. Most of us are of Gentile origin, and but for the incorporation of non-Jewish believers into the Church we would have been left permanently on the outside. We are the beneficiaries of the breakdown of the old barriers. It surely therefore ill behoves us to set up new barriers of our own.

Peter, the apostle who earlier had great problems accepting non-Jews into the Church, takes this further in his Epistle:

But you are a chosen people, a royal priesthood, a holy nation, a people belonging to God, that you may declare the praises of him who called you out of darkness into his wonderful light. Once you were not a people, but now you are the people of God...

Dear friends, I urge you, as aliens and strangers in the world, to abstain from sinful desires, which war against your soul. (1 Peter 2.9–11)

Once the people of Israel were commanded by God to be good to the aliens in their midst. Now Peter says, in effect, that *we* as Christians are the aliens. On becoming Christians, we join a nation whose citizenship is in heaven, and whose loyalty is to God. I think that what Peter wrote has wider ramifications than just being good neighbours to those of different ethnic groups. He is telling us about who we are as Christians, and how we ought to see ourselves.

We know from Paul and Peter, in their epistles, that we should be loyal to the secular ruling authorities. But where, as Christians, does our *ultimate* loyalty lie? To whom do we ultimately belong? Is it to our country, however good that might be? Can it be to our fellow citizens of that country? Or is it to God, and to our fellow Christians *worldwide*, of every possible race, colour and ethnicity? Biblically it would seem that it has to be to the latter, to God and to his people, the Church, of which his grace has made us a part.

Hence the real division is not between pure-bred whites and dirty immigrants, as some would have it, but between those who in God's mercy are within the Church and those outside it to whom we proclaim Christ's message in love.

One practical result of this is that the desire of racists to repatriate immigrants, as well as being morally repugnant, always strikes me as odd in this way. If we had not captured their ancestors into slavery, as is the case of the United States, or conquered their ancestral countries as colonies, as is the case with Britain and France, the majority of their present-day descendants would not be living in our countries today. Globalization might have led many people from developing nations to come to the richer West, as it is doing now, but for the most part, the presence of large non-white communities in Western countries is very much a product of white aggression or imperialism in earlier ages.

So, in conclusion for this chapter, if we are to obey the first commandment – to love God – and the second commandment – to love our neighbour as ourselves – we cannot surely allow ourselves any kind of nationalist position.

Our identity is not based upon any nationalist myth, however benign. It is rather one that God himself has given us through his son. Our citizenship is no longer here on earth but with Christ in heaven. This should always be our prime identity. We must love as our neighbours people in our country whatever their ethnic origin, since that is the command of God in the Old Testament as well as in the New.

6

England's Green and Pleasant Land: Can There Be Such a Thing as Christian England?

At the same time as the dramatic developments of the Reformation were happening in Europe, England too was experiencing great changes. But they were different from the popular spiritual movements that we studied in the last chapter.

Henry VIII was keen to get rid of the power of the Pope in England in order to divorce Catherine and marry Anne, but he expected the Church of England still to hold to Catholic doctrine. Diarmaid MacCulloch's research has shown that so far as thoroughgoing *spiritual* change was concerned, the Reformation did not really get under way in England until the reign of Edward VI. Even then there were still many areas of England where people held to the old beliefs. This was why it was so easy for Mary Tudor to re-impose Catholicism when she succeeded Edward in 1553. None of the rebellions against her was successful, and modern writers have enjoyed imagining history as it might have been, with Mary and her husband Philip of Spain having a child and English Protestantism remaining suppressed permanently.

Until well into Elizabeth's reign, the survival of the Reformation in England was precarious. To a very large extent, the Reformation hung by a thread, and that was the life and continued rule of Elizabeth. It was the assassination of her Catholic cousin Mary Queen of Scots, the triumph of the Reformation in Scotland and the failure of the Armada in 1588 that made the difference – along with Elizabeth's ability to survive normally fatal illnesses so that she was able to reign for forty-five years. By the time she died in 1603 the nation defined itself in very large measure by its Protestant identity.

The fact that Elizabeth became Queen at all was because of her father's marriage to her mother Anne Boleyn, something in itself only made possible by Henry's break with Rome. In turn this meant that the Catholic powers of Europe, France and Spain, did not recognize her as Queen because, so far as they and the Pope were concerned, she was illegitimate. This is why she spent most of her reign under threat either of rebellion in favour of her Catholic cousin, or, after Mary's death, of foreign invasion. Catholicism was thus associated with political powers that wished to overthrow the monarch and substitute someone favourable to foreign interests. To be Catholic was to be unpatriotic, and to be Protestant was to be a loyal subject of the Queen. Protestantism and patriotic Englishness went hand in glove.

However, although she was a Protestant, Elizabeth was above all a politician. England had been ruled by thoroughgoing Calvinist Protestants under Edward, and then by Protestant-burning Catholics under Mary (whose husband Philip tried to dissuade her from such gruesome action as he knew how unpopular it would be). If Elizabeth were to be secure on the throne, she needed to have a Church of England that was Protestant, but not *too* Protestant. After the religious upheavals of the two previous reigns, with their violent fluctuations in policy, she did not want to upset the delicate political/theological apple cart.

AN EVANGELICAL PUZZLE

As a result, the Church of England under Elizabeth became a careful compromise, those of firm views often being excluded by those who trod a cautious middle path. The Puritans, the forerunners both of the American Pilgrims and of many of today's British Evangelicals, were entirely kept from power.

England was a Protestant nation, but it was also one in which those members of the Church of England whose theology was informed by the more overtly Protestant Reformation in Germany or Switzerland were not allowed to play an active role in the formation of doctrine or in the national leadership of the Church.

One result of this was the Pilgrim Fathers, people who took their faith seriously and wanted nothing more than to be able to worship God in a freedom that was denied them by the state and religious authorities.

This is why I am always puzzled by English Evangelicals who make such play today of the fact that we are an officially Protestant country, with a sovereign who is the nominal head of the Established Church. Theologically such people surely have far more in common with their Puritan antecedents. Yet the Puritans either had to flee to the New World or, in the case of those who stayed behind, survive only to be expelled *en masse* from the Church of England soon after the restoration of King Charles II. The one time when Puritan theology prevailed was during the Commonwealth of 1649–60, when the Church of England was abolished and England was a Republic.

My surprise is reinforced by the fact that I am a member of a Church of England church, one with whose theology Cranmer would have felt entirely at home. It represents the kind of Anglican Church that would have prevailed had the spiritual Reformation in the reign of Edward VI lasted for longer and been able to produce a more doctrine-based Church than the compromise version that Elizabeth eventually imposed. My church is also one that is steeped in Puritan heritage, with ties to such outstanding Puritan preachers as Richard Sibbes.

WHAT MAKES A COUNTRY CHRISTIAN?

English Christians need to ask themselves a very fundamental question: *What makes a country Christian?* I will ask another, perhaps even more profound question for American readers, lest they become complacent because of their separation of Church and State! This is: *Can you even have such a thing as a Christian country?*

What makes you a Christian was at the heart of the Reformation. Up until then it had, to no small extent, been a question of birth. You were born into a European country under the authority of the Pope. (I am here ignoring those Orthodox countries under their own Patriarchs, since they were not directly affected by the Reformation.) This geographic/spiritual unity was called Christendom and, as many writers have shown, this unity was rent asunder by Luther. Thereafter, faith effectively ceased to be a matter of birth or geography and far more an issue of belief. You cannot by definition be *physically* born as a born-again Christian, because becoming a Christian is something that, according to the Protestant view, happens *after* your birth, even if you are a practising Christian at a very young age. This is why many Protestant countries, after decades of religious war and much bloodshed, rediscovered the more ancient Christian doctrine of toleration. If becoming a Christian is a voluntary act, or as the late-seventeenth-century philosopher John Locke described it, one of inward change, then no amount of external coercion or inquisition can make any real difference.

This is not to say that all Protestant countries either agreed with Locke or fully implemented such changes – and it was arguably not until the nominally Catholic Napoleon Bonaparte began to rule much of Europe in the early nineteenth century that widespread religious tolerance prevailed. But I think my observation that true freedom did not come until the arrival of the Napoleonic Empire is generally true, with notable exceptions such as the Austrian ruler Joseph II, a Catholic monarch who gave toleration to his Protestant subjects.

So if geography no longer makes a country Christian, as was believed by the inhabitants of Christendom in the Middle Ages, what does?

I'M ENGLISH, SO I'M C OF E

There are plenty of people who say 'I'm English, so I'm C of E'. I would often like to ask what exactly that means. Does it imply, for example, that they would be Catholic in Spain or a Baptist in America (not, of course, that that is a direct analogy)? In that instance, they would still be professing Christians, albeit of a different sort. They certainly profess to be Christian, but they let their form of Christianity be decided not by doctrine but by geography.

On the other hand, it can, with some, mean that they would be Buddhist if born in Thailand or Hindu if raised in India. It is legitimate to ask what such people understand by Christianity.

It is also true that few people always agree in every detail and at all times with whatever denomination they might find themselves belonging to. For example, I am more sympathetic with the theology that states that those who are baptized should already be professing believers, despite my attendance at an Anglican church. But at least my choice of where to go on Sunday is mainly determined by the doctrines and practice of that particular parish, rather than because I live in England.

By way of compromise, many of my fellow Anglicans, while feeling that they ought to attend the official local representative of English Christianity, nevertheless worship at a parish church with whose liturgy and style of churchmanship they feel at home. Furthermore, at least that means that they *do* attend, and do have some kind of actual belief.

One suspects that many of those who say that they are Church of England because they are English are, in reality, rarely seen in any parish church, except perhaps at Easter or Christmas. If that is the case, what species of Christianity is it that they are professing? Is it perhaps more a statement of patriotism, of standing up for and making an outward (but seldom observed) statement of allegiance to one of the country's most famous symbols, its national Church? That of course might be regarded as unfair by many of the notional Anglicans to whom it applies, especially since some of them have some kind of vestigial belief in something, however attenuated it might be in practice.

AN HISTORICALLY AWKWARD QUESTION

Here I would ask some awkward questions of those whose nationalism takes the form of praising England's position as a Christian country, while at the same time they espouse the strong doctrinal beliefs of sixteenth-century Latimer or Ridley, or nineteenth-century Bishop Ryle.

If we look at history, the existence of an established Church of England, with a monarch who has sworn at the coronation to uphold it, has sometimes been of scant comfort to those who held firmly to the doctrines of the Reformers. When the Church of England was restored in 1660 (and similarly the Church of Scotland), there followed a period of violent persecution. In England, the most famous victim was the great John Bunyan, author of *The Pilgrim's Progress*, who was to spend twelve years in prison for his Protestant but non-Anglican beliefs. Over the border in Scotland, the Covenanters were even more severely persecuted, some even losing their lives. The reign of Charles II (1660–85) was also probably one of the most actively immoral periods in English history.

One can argue therefore that the mere fact of Establishment, and of the newly crowned King's or Queen's coronation oath, does not in itself make any difference to the spiritual health of a nation. It is perhaps also insulting to the many thousands of non-Anglican Christians, of all generations, who have also been a very considerable witness to the cause of historic Christianity over the centuries. But most seriously, I cannot help thinking that such a view fails completely to understand what the Reformation view of Christianity and Christian conversion was all about.

Luther himself did not fully grasp the long-term later consequences of what he was preaching. While he believed that conversion was a matter of faith, not of birth or geography, he himself did not see the ultimate result this would have on Church–state relations. Indeed, he was most vigorously opposed to the Anabaptists and to similar radical groups who argued for a total separation between the two. Many Lutheran countries have state churches to this very day, and in his German homeland the state still has close ties with the Lutheran Church.

Ultimately, though, I would like to argue that the situation in the USA, where there is full separation and where church attendance is very considerably higher than in England, is one closer to the situation in which the early Christians found themselves. Not only did the infant Church have no state support, but it had, by contrast, intense opposition and active persecution. Likewise, in our own day, the churches in China have grown exponentially in size, despite decades of vigorous government hostility and, after 1951, the expulsion of most of the Western missionaries.

If conversion is an individual thing, what difference does it make what country it takes place in? Why should establishment influence what people do spiritually, if there is no correlation between church growth and a formal state Church? This is especially the case as the churches seem to be more active in countries where there is separation or even outright persecution, such as the USA and much of Africa in the first case, and China in the second.

While it is gratifying that the present Queen is widely believed to take her beliefs seriously, one can hardly say that the majority of her predecessors were people whose lives have made any difference at all to the spiritual life of the nation. Yet they too took the same coronation oath to uphold the established Church by which many English Christians set great store.

Furthermore, one suspects that many, who with arguably good cause praise Elizabeth II, will have serious problems when we have King Charles III, who has said that he will not be a Defender of *the* Faith, the title borne since King Henry VIII, but the Defender of *Faith* in general. While that tolerance is laudable in a multi-faith and multiracial society, it also betokens the kind of spiritual relativism that goes against all the claims of Christ to be the unique path to salvation.

In conclusion, those who laud the particular position of England have, in effect, to say two things.

JESUS AND THE PHARISEES

First, they have to argue that while no mention of God blessing countries exists in the New Testament, God nonetheless still sees countries in the Christian era in the way that he saw the Children of Israel in Old Testament times. (We will revisit this issue when we examine the United States, where it is also very relevant, and when we consider Cromwell's rule in England.)

However, when we looked at how God saw Israel in the Old Covenant, we noticed that his relationship with them was closely linked with their *spiritual* relationship with him and not just their blood descent from Abraham. As John the Baptist pointed out to the Pharisees and Sadducees, accident of birth makes no difference to one's relationship to God:

> You brood of vipers! Who warned you to flee from the coming wrath? Produce fruit in keeping with repentance. And do not think that you can say to yourselves, 'We have Abraham as our father.' I tell you that out of these stones God can raise up children for Abraham. (Matthew 3.7–9; also Luke 3. 7–8)

As Jesus himself told them:

> I know you are Abraham's descendants. Yet you are ready to kill me, because you have no room for my word... If you were Abraham's children... then you would do the things Abraham did. As it is, you are determined to kill me, a man who has told you the truth that I heard from God. Abraham did not do such things. (John 8.37, 39–40)

If being Jewish made no difference to salvation when Christ was here on earth, how can being English (or any other nationality) possibly make a difference today? The Pharisees and Sadducees were the official religious establishment of their day yet, as we know, they were to go on to reject Jesus as the Messiah and put him to death.

AN UNFAIR ADVANTAGE OF GEOGRAPHY?

Second, such a view implies that God gives an unfair advantage to people because of accident of geography. This works itself out in many different ways. For instance, there are great and godly Christians who believe that God preserved Britain especially from Nazi conquest in 1940. It is certainly a relief that all but the

Channel Islands were spared German occupation during the Second World War, and we can all be thankful to God that we did not suffer the same fate as so many countries during that period.

On the other hand, do we or can we believe that Britain, Sweden and Switzerland, all of which avoided conquest, are somehow more godly countries than places such as Norway, Denmark or the Netherlands, all of which have rich Protestant heritages, and which did suffer occupation and conquest? Here one can add that Sweden and Switzerland escaped through being neutral – perhaps not a great recommendation. How much was Britain's escape due to her island geography? I suspect that the answer to that is 'a great deal'.

Otherwise one would have to say that God looks upon, for example, Bangladesh in special judgement. This is because Bangladesh is prone to so much natural catastrophe and flooding. According to this logic, why is God not also angry with, say, Pakistan, which is an equally Muslim country in the Indian sub-continent but escapes such regular cataclysms?

It does seem strange to base theology on escaping the ill-fortune of others. It also seems to suggest that if you are born in the right country, God is more likely to look favourably upon you because of the deeds of godly people of centuries gone by. If, however, one looks at conversion growth, it would seem that God is richly blessing many countries in Africa and Asia, areas of the world that do not have a long history of Christian faith, rather than places such as the United Kingdom or the Netherlands, that do. The problem in many parts of sub-Saharan Africa is that they cannot train ministers fast enough to catch up with the numbers of people becoming Christians, which is sadly no longer the case in the West.

Finally, if one looks at the New Testament, it does seem that there is no longer a division on the grounds of nation but between those who accept the offer of salvation in Christ and those who do not. Both these categories of people are multiracial and multi-ethnic, since both the Church and those who reject the gospel stem from every nation under the sun. A Nigerian or

Peruvian who is a Christian is *spiritually* in an infinitely more privileged position than an English person who is not. Since church growth in both the former areas is far outstripping the decline in the West, England included, one can say that people in those countries are more privileged. The reason is that they are more likely to hear the gospel clearly presented to them than those in nations where Christian faith is no longer so strong.

SO WHAT DOES MAKE A COUNTRY CHRISTIAN?

What makes a country Christian? Surely it is not history, since otherwise many West European states would see an increase in those becoming practising Christians, rather than the reverse. The fact of Establishment seems not to make much difference either. Historically it can lead to Christians being persecuted, as in the days of Bunyan.

In terms of demography, especially if, as in Britain, adherents of the established Church are only a part of the actively church-going Christian community, one cannot say that state privilege makes the difference. People are becoming Christians through Baptist, Methodist, House Church and numerous other non-Anglican forms of belief and, if the statistics are credible, *more* so than through the Church of England.

One can also argue that those Anglican churches that are growing, such as the one my wife and I attend, are those that, doctrinally, probably have much more in common with non-conformist churches that take Scripture seriously than those Anglican parishes that do not. If this is true, as I suspect that it might be, this means that it is not the established nature of such churches that causes them to grow, but their theological orientation, which has nothing to do with being part of a state Church. In Cambridge, for example, which has an unusually high rate of regular church attendance, all those churches contributing six-figure sums to the local diocese as part of their parish share would fall into this doctrinal category.

Interestingly enough, what also marks out these Cambridge parishes is the strongly international flavour of their congregations.

The parishioners come from literally all over the globe, in many cases from those same Third World countries in which Christianity is growing so fast. This too would indicate that it is their theology, rather than anything traditionally or quintessentially English about their liturgy, that is at the heart of the reasons people attend them.

If one has to judge the spiritual health of nations by the proportion of those in active Christian practice, as opposed to some loose form of nominal adherence, then the countries of Western Europe, Britain included, would rank very low on the list. Some who regard England as a Christian country would readily content themselves with outward conformity or notional allegiance. But surely those who are Evangelical would have stricter criteria, and on *those* grounds it would not begin to be possible to describe England as a Christian country.

HOW ABOUT PROPHETIC CLAIMS OR VISIONS ABOUT ENGLAND?

There are sincere Christians who base much of their theology of how God regards Britain on visions or prophecies. Since this is a book on nationalism and religious myth, this is not really the place to cast theological judgement on whether such claims can be said to have any scriptural or other validity. I should also add that for many readers of this book, the paragraphs that follow will either be meaningless or bizarre. But since it is a very crucial issue for many other Christians, it is one with which we ought to deal.

For those for whom it is an issue, it is important to say that many leading theologians of charismatic or Pentecostal sympathy, in Britain and the USA, would always insist on employing biblical methods of testing whether or not such prophecies are true. This would be the case regardless of the Christian commitment of the person giving the prophecy.

It should also be said that most Evangelical Christians would feel very uneasy about making such important theological statements on the basis of prophecies, even presuming that they are part of the Evangelical community which regards such gifts as still in existence. Even within the charismatic end of the Evangelical spectrum, there is no final agreement on what defines a present-day prophecy. To the majority of Evangelicals, if such a gift does continue it is in preaching the Sunday sermon, and is nothing like as dramatic as a direct word from God himself.

So even from a charismatic or Pentecostal perspective it is very hard to think of any New Testament grounds that would come anywhere near validating prophecies that God has a particular or special role for England or anywhere else. As we have seen, the overwhelming emphasis of Scripture is that the only division that exists is that between Christians and non-Christians.

That is not to say that God does not have a plan for history. Whichever of the numerous interpretations one takes for the Book of Revelation, it is clear that God is still profoundly involved in the historical process. But it is also evident from Revelation – again regardless of any specific interpretation – that that book is about God's plan for salvation and his plan for his people. Since Christ, God's people have not been a physical nation but the multinational Church.

Even those who believe in ongoing prophecy would therefore need to recognize the biblical insistence on all prophetic utterance being properly tested. With the scriptural division of everyone into *spiritual* and not national categories, it would seem very difficult for those believing in the continuation of the miraculous-sign gifts to accept without question any pronouncement that God still has a specific purpose for the English *as a nation*.

That is not to say that God has no purpose for those hundreds of thousands of people who make active profession of Christian faith and who happen to live in England. He certainly does! But it is because they are his sons and daughters in Christ, and not because of where they live. God is mightily and evidently at work around his world, and that is something in which we can all rejoice. Surely that is far more exciting than the fate of a small offshore island?

BRITAIN AND THE BEAST? WHY I AM NOT
DEALING HERE WITH THE EU

In this particular book, I am not dealing with an issue that vexes many British Christians, namely that of the United Kingdom's membership of the European Union. This is dealt with at proper length and in due biblical depth by Fred Catherwood's book *Pro-Europe*. Suffice it to say here that I am always puzzled when I read comments such as 'As Christians, we are of course against large political institutions.' Such statements are usually implicitly accepted in the articles or books in which they appear. But on what *scriptural* grounds can one make such a statement?

The People's Republic of China is an enormous state and the most populated in the world. Yet consider the phenomenal church growth in that country – does any part of Britain see such increase in conversions? If Europe is evil, what does that make the USA, which is far bigger geographically and in every other way than the European Union? Yet it is arguably the most actively Christian country on earth. How can size be something that Christians are instinctively against, when two such giants of nation states are seeing such evidence of God at work amidst his people?

This is surely why we need to test *all* of our opinions in terms of our doctrine, since it is all too easy to baptize our prejudices and disguise them in Christian garb. I am sure that those who disagree with me on the issue of Britain and the European Union will say that I am doing just that! But I would ask them: on what *scriptural* basis do you hold the views that you do? One of the purposes of this book is to try to separate national myth from proper Christian belief, and this kind of issue is a classic example of where I think the two things very easily get hopelessly confused.

In the next chapter, we will look at the United States, an enormous country that has a very high percentage of practising Christians. We will consider the relationship between its founding and its Christian present, and whether or not those two things have anything to do with one another.

7

How Christian Was the Founding of America?

Many of the issues we have discussed hitherto might seem irrelevant to Christians in the USA, where there is no established Church about which to argue. However, I do not think that it is as simple as that. In this chapter, therefore, we will look in more detail at specifically American issues. They show that even though America does have separation of Church and state, not all Christians – either in the United States or in Britain – appreciate that this could be a blessing.

WHO LOST AMERICA?

There are several debates in the USA, some of which have been part of the heated controversies of the past thirty years that are often called the *culture wars*. Much of this has been overtly political, and is inexorably linked to the rise of the Christian Right and such movements as the Moral Majority. This is something about which much has been written, and I do not want to duplicate what has been covered in far more detail elsewhere. As well as the fact that it is meaningless to non-American readers of this book, it is a subject that is so polarizing that to touch it would be very unwise!

However, some of these arguments are about the history of the USA, and the role played by religion both in the colonial period and in the years up to and immediately after American independence in 1776. Here I think I might just be brave enough to speak. So let us look first at the history itself, and then at the theological implications, the source of much of the current debate. In essence, many American Christians feel that whereas in the past there was a societal outlook favourable to Christian values, that has now vanished. As Mark Noll has said, some Evangelicals feel that their America has been stolen from them.

It is not only hard-line right wingers who proclaim such a view; other serious Evangelical leaders have felt the same way. But their view is based on a false historical premise, and they therefore undermine the excellent *biblical* case for American Evangelicals to get involved in society as salt and light. Since on *that* issue serious American Christians are scripturally correct, it has always struck me as regrettable that they used so historically shaky an argument to make their case not just to their fellow Evangelicals but also to American society at large. Many secular historians, who examined what *actually* happened in the history of the USA, were able to point out the mistakes in the historical analysis by those Evangelicals who made them. Some of these critics then went further and rejected the notion that Christianity played any role at all in the infant republic; Evangelical scholars at well-respected American universities have been able to show that this is equally mistaken. Their first battle is against those who ascribe no role to religion, and their other, regrettably, is to fellow Evangelicals who ascribe far too much.

A NEW WORLD?

One of the best-known American festivities worldwide is Thanksgiving. It is the commemoration of the first harvest of the pilgrims in the New World. These early settlers, in what is now Massachusetts, were Puritan refugees from religious repression back at home in England. They were doubly thankful – not just for the success of the harvest, but that God had preserved their lives in what was still, for Europeans, an inhospitable land. So while Americans of all descriptions now celebrate Thanksgiving, its origins are profoundly Christian.

So far, what I have written is indisputable. But it is here that the myths begin. The first is that the Pilgrims, and other Puritans crossing the Atlantic to the New World, were typical of the new Americans. This is wrong in many ways.

To begin with, the Europeans were by no means the first peoples to come to North America. The Native American peoples, entering from the other side of the continent, from Asia across the Bering Straits, had already been in the region for thousands of years, not to speak of possible early Viking and other similar abortive settlements. Nor were the Pilgrims the first Europeans: the Spaniards had also arrived, in places like Florida, and they were Catholics seeking to extend their Empire, not Protestants seeking new life and liberty.

Perhaps more importantly, the Pilgrims and their like were not the only British immigrants either. My wife is descended from some of the earliest settlers in Virginia, which is a colony as old and eminent as New England.

Virginia was settled with official support and as a financial venture. While many of the new Virginians were professing Christians, they were in the New World to make money, not to find freedom. The Governor was a royal appointee; the Church of England, from which the Puritans were fleeing, was established in the new colony; and the colony itself was a microcosm of the social order back in England. While many of the colonial gentry were respectable Anglicans, they were independent-minded individuals for whom religion played a formal but distant role. (The research of distinguished Baptist historian John S. Moore is invaluable here.)

THE REALITIES OF EARLY COLONIAL AMERICA

Another important point to remember is that while the Puritans were getting away from persecution at home, they were not trying to set up a colony in which religious freedom as we understand it was crucial or even existed. They were strongly influenced by covenant theology, in which the political establishment played a key role. Just as God had covenants with his people Israel in the Old Testament, so, they believed, God continued to have covenants with his Christian people thereafter. This meant that what the Pilgrim Fathers and others were doing was *not* to set up a society in which everyone could worship God freely as they chose. What was wrong with the England they were leaving was not so much that it lacked freedom, but that the establishment was theologically in error.

One of the biggest influences on the early Puritans was their view of the Second Coming of Christ – their *eschatology* or theology of the end of time. This played a key historical role and Americans continue to be fascinated by the subject (novels such as the *Left Behind* series, with an eschatological theme, still sell in millions). I am not taking any eschatological sides in this book! Apart from the dangers of doing so, the truth or otherwise of the different theories is not relevant to my argument; what matters is what was done by people who believed in them in the past, like the Puritans.

Nowadays, we would probably call their view *postmillennial.* Based upon their understanding of the Book of Revelation, they believed that Christ would come to earth, for his second and final coming, after the reign of godly people for a thousand years (*post* = after, *millennium* = thousand). In this understanding of eschatology, it was possible, they felt, to help the return of Christ along by establishing a state in which Christ was both followed and worshipped properly.

Postmillennialism has been called the optimistic version of events because, unlike its *pre-millennial* rival, in which things get worse before Christ returns, in the postmillennial theory the Church ends up triumphant for a thousand years before Christ's coming again.

Although the Puritans' writings show that they loved life as much as anyone else, they have usually been sadly caricatured as a rather dour lot. I think that their eschatology shows them to be the opposite. It must have been very exciting being out there in the belief that what you were doing was making a real *spiritual* difference. How much of America's famous 'can-do' spirit comes from the sense of theological optimism and excitement brought to the New World by the early Puritans? While a similar optimistic outlook pervades the wholly secular foundation of Australia ('no worries'), I cannot help feeling that the wholesome, positive side of American life owes much to the similar but spiritually rooted sense of achievement of the early settlers in New England.

However, there was also a strong down side to what they were soon calling the 'New England way'.

THE DOWN SIDE OF THE NEW ENGLAND WAY

The Salem witch trials have become immortalized in literature. I think what is actually truly remarkable is how *few* poor innocent women were executed in contrast to the proportionately far higher numbers back over in continental Europe. Furthermore, many of those involved in prosecuting the 'witches' later deeply regretted their actions.

What is more worrying, and is more relevant to the theme of our book, is the fact that Quakers also were put to death for nothing other than their beliefs. New England was not the great beacon of religious liberty that we suppose. A persecuting Anglican establishment in England was replaced by an equally persecuting Congregationalist Puritan establishment in places such as Massachusetts, not to mention a persecuting Anglican establishment in Virginia.

This means that both in New England, which consisted of essentially self-regulating colonies such as Massachusetts, and in the South, where there were crown colonies such as Virginia and the two Carolinas, religious establishments existed where complete religious freedom was *not* allowed.

It was in the mid-Atlantic colonies where true religious toleration existed. In the Rhode Island of Roger Williams, the famous dissenter, and above all the Pennsylvania of William Penn, religious pluralism *did* exist, as it also did for a while in the Catholic foundation of Maryland.

THE SPIRITUAL IMPORTANCE OF THE
HALF-WAY COVENANT

There was also a strong spiritual down side even in Massachusetts, known as the *half-way covenant*, to which I alluded earlier. In Puritan covenant theology, the children of believing Christians had a place within the church – as they still do in Presbyterian churches today. In New England this was also political, since you had to be a full church member in order to vote. Here it is important to say that the states of New England were not theocracies – they were not ruled by the local clergy. But the people in charge politically were all members of the established congregational churches, and so while there was no direct rule by the clerical establishment, nonetheless both Church and state were inexorably linked in terms of power.

As we saw, the initial Pilgrims were full of active spiritual enthusiasm: they were there because they believed something. But, of course, one of the basic tenets of the Reformation is that you cannot inherit your faith – as we put it today, God has no grandchildren. If you become a Christian through the new birth, that is something personal between you and God. You do not and cannot inherit this faith from your parents.

So in time, later generations of New Englanders drifted away from a personal faith. However, many in this category had been the children of believing parents, and thus within the existing covenant. While they were not strong believers, they wanted their children brought into the covenant of church membership, since this brought political rights and full membership of society as a whole. Church and colonial leaders realized therefore that they now had a problem. So they established half-way church membership – the *half-way covenant*. Consequently, the children of half-hearted members would have some kind of membership without being admitted in full.

The fact that this was as early as 1662 shows that it had not taken very long for the early spiritual enthusiasm of the founding fathers to become seriously diluted. That is not to say that New

England did not contain within it thousands of people who sincerely believed their faith. But it does suggest that the dream of the Pilgrims of an entirely Christian commonwealth was already in trouble.

Then because of events in England, direct rule was imposed on all the colonies, New England included, at the end of the seventeenth century. This meant even more than before that godly rule was now going to be impossible to sustain, since governors from England certainly could not be relied upon to maintain it.

EIGHTEENTH-CENTURY AMERICA AND THE NEED FOR REVIVAL

By the eighteenth century, the American colonies as a whole could not be said to be the bright shining light, the city upon the hill, longed for by the early Christian settlers. This was something recognized by leaders such as Cotton Mather, the author of countless books, and *The Great Works of Christ in America* in particular. He understood that many of the inhabitants of the colonies were nominal in their faith, if they professed it at all.

This sense of spiritual malaise led to one of the most famous Christian revivals in history – the Great Awakening. While this is often written about in a purely American context, I think one can look at it as a transatlantic phenomenon. One of the mightiest preachers involved in it was George Whitefield, whose powerful evangelism was as widespread in his home country of England as it was in the American colonies.

Within New England itself, the Great Awakening produced one of America's most revered Christians, the great Jonathan Edwards, a Congregational minister but also a mighty intellectual whose legacy at Yale University is still a source of study today. Edwards was, despite the amazing spiritual harvest, removed from his church in Northampton, Massachusetts, since many of the Congregational establishment opposed both him and the Awakening. This was because they, like their English counterparts in their encounters with the early Methodists, disliked what they called the over-enthusiasm brought about by the spiritual experiences of so many of the Awakening's converts. But despite such lack of official support, the Awakening spread to all the parts of the colonies we discussed earlier – the originally Puritan North East (or New England), the mid-Atlantic states, and the Anglican South.

THE AMERICAN DECLARATION OF INDEPENDENCE: HOW CHRISTIAN WAS IT?

Inevitably, some of the enthusiasm had dissipated over the decades between the Awakening and the crisis between Britain and her colonies that led to American independence.

Much ink was spilt in the culture wars of the 1990s in America on how Christian were the founders of the new American republic. Being a British outsider, I shall tread here with much caution. There are some observations I can make, however, since I am following the views of many contemporary American historians. They include, for example, Mark Noll, whose Evangelical credentials are as impeccable as his scholarship.

All this is important, because what happened at this time is all part of the claim by some present-day American Christians that their country was once Christian and was robbed of its Christian heritage by secular humanists in the twentieth century. I also think that when we look at the past, an important *theological* observation needs to be made, in conjunction with making the necessary historical judgements.

At the beginning of the nineteenth century, the newly independent Americans experienced what historians now call the Second Great Awakening. Quite apart from its spiritual impact, it had a massive and permanent effect on the denominational composition of the United States. Some of this, as we shall soon see, was because of the new separation of Church and State introduced by the First Amendment to the Constitution. But in changing the denominational patterns of America, it also changed the theological language in which Christian belief was expressed.

This means that reading late-twentieth- and early-twenty-first-century theology back into that of the late eighteenth is not always easy. How can you tell who was *then* the equivalent of a present-day Evangelical? One eminent American historian has written, for example, that only one of the framers of the American constitution could today be described as an Evangelical. This kind of language creates all kinds of dispute, because those wishing to see the direct hand of God in the forming of the new Republic tend to regard statements like this as hostile to the Christian faith, even though that is far from the intent of the author.

Historically, such a claim does leave out Witherspoon, a Scottish Presbyterian who was – this is indisputable – the only ordained clergyman among the Constitution's framers. It also omits someone whose views were not unlike those of contemporary Evangelicals: Patrick Henry, an Anglican from Virginia.

However, I tend to agree with those Evangelical historians at mainstream American colleges that the overwhelming preponderance of view among the leading founders was what is called *deist*. This was a loose form of Christianity that was certainly more influenced by the prevailing secular outlook of the European Enlightenment than it was by any form of historic Christian faith, let alone that of the Great Awakening.

This would be especially true of the intellectual fathers of the American Revolution, Thomas Jefferson and Benjamin Franklin, both of whom made life easier for historians by putting their views in writing. But it is also arguably true of the great first President himself, George Washington. While he would have described himself as a Christian, his church attendance was distinctly irregular and his theological views, inasmuch as they existed at all, could be safely called fairly nondescript.

THE FIRST AMENDMENT AND THE SEPARATION OF CHURCH AND STATE

Not long after the formal founding of the Republic, it was felt necessary to introduce some amendments, now known as the Bill of Rights. Among these was the First Amendment, which made it clear that the infant state would not have any form of established religion.

However, what is forgotten by both Christians and anti-Christians alike is that when this was passed in 1791, five of the states *did* have an established Church, and seven more had religious tests of some kind for holding office. Incidentally, the Jewish population of Pennsylvania did not complain that such religious tests existed in their state – what irked them was that as you had to believe in *both* Testaments, that excluded them as they rejected the New Testament!

In other words, Christians in the USA today have a completely fair point when they say that it was not the intention of the Founding Fathers to exclude religion altogether from the public sphere, as many secularists would claim. There is nothing unconstitutional about people in public life taking note of the spiritual dimension of life, nor should it be thought somehow illegal if Christians want to hold private prayer meetings on public property. All these are fully compatible with what the framers of the First Amendment had in mind.

The problem that they had was that there was no consensus on what the form of established religion should be, were there to be one. Choose that of one state, and you alienated those following another equally valid form of Christian faith in another. So, as Mark Noll has suggested, they solved the problem in effect by running away from it and deciding that the Congress would have no established faith.

This did not mean that no *individual* in public life could be actively religious. But what it did imply was that, unlike in England, for example, where Anglicans were privileged over dissenters, such a person could not give his version of the faith domination over those of others.

As with this whole issue of the place of Christianity in American public life, much ink has been spilt trying to find a theological rationale for their decision. Here it is more difficult, as not everyone wrote down their reasons.

A JEFFERSONIAN CONUNDRUM

With Thomas Jefferson it is much easier, since in 1785 he had been instrumental in getting complete liberty of worship in his home state of Virginia, which had hitherto been part of the Anglican establishment. For him, everyone, whether Christian, Muslim or Hindu should have exactly the same freedom – a position which reflected his own spiritual outlook.

Some Christians have problems with this, feeling that as Christianity is true, it should have some kind of official state recognition. Although I am myself a firm believer in the absolute exclusive truth of the Christian faith, I have considerable theological misgivings with such a point of view, and do so *because* I am an practising Christian rather than despite it. I am what you could describe as an Evangelical believer in the separation of Church and state, despite, as I mentioned earlier, being a very happy member of an excellent Church of England parish!

This is because if one looks at Scripture, while there is a very clear role given to the state (in epistles like Paul to the Romans, or First Peter), the defence of God's truth is not among them! It is for God's *Church*, his people on earth, to defend the gospel, and not the state, even though the institution of the state is clearly ordained by God himself.

Furthermore, it is very evident that God does not need a friendly state for his Church to grow, as is shown by the exponential growth in its first three centuries, and in countries such as China in the twentieth.

Not only that, but how do Christian believers get the state to defend the kind of Christianity in which they believe? To me, one of the ironies of the situation in the USA is that it is often my fellow Evangelicals who are keenest on things like prayer in schools and other such symbolic issues designed to bring Christian faith back into the centre of public attention. Surely the example of Britain, with an established church and daily prayer in schools, but with a considerably lower percentage of church attendance, shows the errors of such thinking?

Prayer in British schools now reflects Britain's multicultural identity, often containing Hindu or Muslim prayers as well as Christian. This is why some British Evangelicals take the opposite point of view from their American equivalents – they want prayer in schools abolished rather than introduced! We have hundreds of government-funded Church of England, Roman Catholic and similar schools in the United Kingdom, but proportionately far fewer Christians as well.

If we want church leaders to stand up for the truth as we believe it, it is odd to rely on politicians to choose them for us, as happens with the Church of England in the United Kingdom. How could Evangelicals guarantee that it was their version of Christianity that prevailed if the United States were to grant public recognition of Christian faith?

Would it not be more likely to be a watered down, lowest common denominator variant of Christianity, which might please more establishment-minded mainstream denomination leaders in America, but not at all the Evangelical constituency that wants it? In which case, why try to have it at all? At least Christianity would not be associated with the kind of woolly thinking that makes so many active British Christians moan whenever a Church of England bishop makes a pronouncement denying some long-held Christian position.

A MOSQUE IN LONDON FOR A CATHEDRAL IN CAIRO?

One of the main themes of this book is also that we should be global Christians; ours is a worldwide faith, encompassing all ethnic groups and nations. We ought therefore always to think of what effects our actions in our own countries have on our brothers and sisters in Christ who live in nations where the kind of tolerance given in the USA does not exist. In particular, with the dangers of growing tension between the Islamic world and the West, we should be especially mindful of the consequences for our fellow Christians living in predominantly Muslim countries.

One of the ways in which Muslims attack the West is that they say it is both decadent and Christian. After 11 September 2001 even secular news journals such as the *Economist* thought it might be worth telling Muslim countries that such states also had within them large Muslim minorities that were able to worship freely. This is all the more important, since Christians do not have anything like the freedom to worship in, say, Saudi Arabia, that a Muslim does in New York.

In particular, so far as this argument is concerned, surely the fact that the USA has within it such a strongly vibrant Christian church without any state support is a strong witness to the claims of the Christian faith. Unlike Muslim nations, which use the coercive power of the state to enforce religious obedience, millions of Americans are active Christians entirely by their own choice and without any official coercion of any kind. Nor does the fact that Muslims are equally free in the USA prevent the Christian church from thriving and growing – it does not need state repression of other faiths in order to do this.

Were Christianity to become an official religion, it would give the Muslims the same grounds for complaint that they legitimately have in the United Kingdom. Britain still has an anti-blasphemy law, but this protects Christianity only.

Muslims now want this law to extend to all faiths, including Islam. Several Christian groups, especially those working evangelistically among Muslims, are deeply concerned. Should such legislation pass, cross-cultural evangelism might become virtually illegal, since Muslims could then complain that such literature was blasphemous in relation to Islamic beliefs. If, on the other hand, the government refuses, then Muslims can say that they are being persecuted in a Christian country.

At the moment, Christians are able to point out to Muslim governments that Christians are persecuted in Muslim countries, but not the other way around. It would be unfortunate were any Western country to give Muslims a chance to say otherwise. Since in the USA no religion of any kind has state protection, and that lack of protection is actually in the Bill of Rights, American Christians are able to say to Muslim regimes that Christians in

Islamic countries should have the same freedom that Muslims do *constitutionally* in the USA.

This was why the partly Christian-owned firm John Laing agreed to build a mosque in London back in the 1970s, despite the opposition of many Christian groups. Their argument was that since we wanted to be able to have freedom for Christians to worship in Egypt, and to build a proper church in Cairo, it was necessary to be able to show the Egyptians that Muslims could worship freely in London. Surely it would be wrong to deny Egyptian Christians the same freedom that British Muslims enjoyed?

This is why the Christian human rights advocacy group Advocates International always stands up for the rights of all believers in any faith to be able to exercise those freedoms as prescribed in the UN Charter. If you want to protect the rights of Christians being persecuted in Turkey, it helps if you have already protected those of Muslims living in Greece, a country that severely restricts the rights of non-Greek Orthodox, whether Muslim, Evangelical Protestant or Roman Catholic. Since the USA grants permission for any religious group, however bizarre, to worship freely, Advocates International (a USA-based organization) is in a very persuasive position to protect the rights of Christians in totalitarian regimes.

The trouble, surely, with those who wish to have an exclusive, established, state-protected church is that they often forget their church history. They lose sight of the power of the faith that they seek to protect. Tyrants such as Nero, Stalin, Hitler and Mao all failed to obliterate the Christians of their time; as the ancient saying goes, the blood of the martyrs is the seed of the Church. How much of a favour did Constantine really do the church of his day when he made it the official religion of the Roman Empire?

Many people who want to have a Christian state live in the USA. Let us now therefore look at how American Christians have so mythologized their Christian past as to create real problems in the present. That will be the theme of the next chapter.

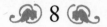

8

Our God Is Too Small:
Can There Ever
Be a Christian Country?

In the last chapter we looked at the foundation myths of America, and the way Christians there have invented a non-existent Christian past. The contention of this chapter will, inevitably, be controversial. I shall argue that such attitudes show a diminished view of the power and sovereignty of God, lacking in biblical support.

THE SPIRITUAL DANGERS OF A MYTHICAL PAST

One of the things that we need to decide is: can there be such a thing as a Christian country? This is, I think, at the heart of the debate that is going on in America and, perhaps to a lesser extent, among those people who hold to similar views in Britain and elsewhere.

We saw when we looked at the Children of Israel in another chapter that simply being born of Jewish parents did not make you *automatically* one of God's people. True faith in God and obedience to his law were essential prerequisites. Many of the founders of New England saw themselves as inaugurating a New (albeit Christian) Israel. Despite their knowledge of the Old Testament, they did not remember that geography did not in itself make for a people of God. Being Protestants, they should also have remembered the Protestant stress on the *new* birth – it is through conversion and not human parentage that you are saved.

As for people in the other colonies, while many of them were surely very godly, they were not there to create a state on earth that could bring in the Millennium. Theirs was an altogether more secular outlook, however much they might have respected the Christian faith and in some cases believed in it. Therefore attempts by present-day Christians to confer a godly status on the American past are, as Mark Noll rightly points out in his many works, based on a mistaken or even fraudulent view of the past.

This is not in any way to cast doubt upon the sincerity of many of the Christians who look back on a mythic Christian America which never existed – or certainly not in the way many Evangelicals now believe. Like Mark Noll and other contemporary American historians such as George Marsden, Nathan Hatch and Harry Stout, I am particularly disturbed by this phenomenon because of my own Evangelical beliefs.

To me (and to writers like Noll), at the heart of Christian faith is the fact of the Cross of Calvary – the message of salvation in Jesus Christ. It is a living faith in that truth which makes someone a Christian. As we saw from the history of the early Church, Christianity did not have and did not need a Christian government or predominantly Christian society in which to grow. It was the message of salvation spread by ordinary Christians in the power of the Holy Spirit that caused the infant Church to grow exponentially across the Roman Empire and beyond.

One of the finest apologists for this message in the twentieth century was Francis Schaeffer, whose life spanned most of it. He and I debated this very issue – some of that correspondence is in his book *The Great Evangelical Disaster*, in which Schaeffer made a prophetic call for Christians to stand up for historic biblical truth. Yet to my surprise, and to that of many of my fellow Evangelicals in Europe, whose lives had been as deeply influenced by him as mine had, even he began to follow this strange and tragically false interpretation of America's past. While it is possible to see the attraction of the myth for those whose political agenda it suited, it struck me as puzzling that someone who understood the *spiritual* realities as acutely as Schaeffer did followed it as well.

Surely the real issue is: *How can you have a Christian country this side of eternity? Can you have a truly Christian country unless all the people in it are Christians, and also without sin?*

To me, the answer is obvious: you cannot. Even if you had a society in which 100 per cent of all its citizens were truly Christian, because we are sinners even that society would not be perfect. This is something which the founders of New England, despite the very realistic attitude towards sin and the spiritual struggle of the Puritans, surely failed to grasp. Here the half-way covenant is surely most revealing, because it is an effective measure of the failure in the real world of the founders' dreams.

CHRISTIANS AS SALT AND LIGHT

Christians in the USA are always astonished when I tell them that there are active Evangelicals in all of the major political parties in Britain. As the old saying went, the British Labour Party was always 'more Methodism than Marx'. This gives British Evangelicals a far larger influence than those in the USA, because they are heard whoever is in power.

In the USA, by contrast, Evangelicals are today almost overwhelmingly in the Republican Party. Issues such as abortion have become highly politicized and thus exceptionally polarized. While this is not the place to get into such complex and controversial issues, it is worth saying that it is often the same people who so misunderstand America's past that are today seeking political rather than spiritual solutions for the nation's moral woes. This is not to question the complete sincerity of those American Christians who, from a non-American perspective, seem to have put their trust in the princes and chariots of today, rather than in the power of the message of salvation to transform the soul as well as the body.

In addition, by linking the eternally true Gospel of Jesus Christ with overt political partisanship, there is the very real danger that your politics will shout so loudly that people do not hear the Good News of salvation that you are also trying to proclaim. If they are switching you off because of what they see as your politically partisan secular views, they will do the same for your spiritual declaration. Since the message of the Cross is one that everyone needs to hear, this is surely tragic.

THE DANGERS OF LINKING THE TRUTH OF
CHRIST TO PARTISAN POLITICS

Is there not also the danger that we baptize our political views, and give them the same status of eternal truth that we do to Scripture? Do we want people to reject God's word because they oppose our political platform? Surely we ought to have the perspective that while we sincerely believe our political views are right, we cannot ascribe to them the absolute truth that we do as Christians to our core spiritual beliefs. We may even not be aware that we are doing this, but that is often how non-Christians hear us. All too often the political check list that Christian groups give out at election time has a lot of very partisan points on it as well as moral issues upon which all Christians can agree.

In terms of American political history, this is very ironic. Today many Republican-voting Evangelicals declare their strong dislike of what they describe as Big Government. Historically this is what much of American history is about – part of the reason for the founding of the USA was a desire of men and women to escape what they felt to be despotic government in the countries from which they emigrated.

From a British viewpoint, it seems hard to justify either actively interventionist government or minimal interference government *as such* on *scriptural* grounds – all would depend on what governments of either stripe actually did or neglected to do.

Historically, the most successful Evangelical Christians in the United States were those described as *formalists*, in the period running up to the Civil War of the 1860s. In particular, these Evangelicals were at the forefront of the abolitionist movement, which campaigned actively, and on Christian grounds, for the abolition of slavery and of the slave trade. In order to achieve this, Big Government was urgently necessary. This happened because it was necessary for the Federal Government in Washington to override the vehement opposition of the slave-owning states, which wished to decide such issues at a local level.

Nowadays, the situation is in fact more complex (as Mark

Noll for one has pointed out). On the one hand, Evangelical Republicans want Federal power, through the Supreme Court, to outlaw abortion, while on the other hand they want that power reduced so that people can live without government interference in their lives.

This puts Evangelicals in the same tradition as those misguided Christians who so opposed Big Government before the Civil War, namely those who believed in States' Rights and in the retention of slavery. Many of the divisions among active Christians today date back to the 1840s, when Christians in the north supported freedom for the slaves, while those in the south supported the institution of slavery, even trying to do so on biblical grounds.

There is also another irony today, pointed out by Catholic commentator E. J. Dionne of the *Washington Post*. President George W. Bush was elected in 2000 as the first Evangelical to go to the White House since Jimmy Carter in 1976. But as a result of the events of 11 September 2001 and the need to defend the homeland adequately against foreign threat, he massively increased the scope of Federal Government power. Yet he was the candidate for whom most white Evangelicals voted.

All this is, surely, not helpful for the cause of Christianity either within the United States or globally. This, I would argue, is because historic Christianity can be caricatured not as a faith with complete relevance to all people at all times in every land, but as an American phenomenon linked to a very particular and often aggressively partisan point of view.

THERE ARE NO GROUNDS FOR BRITISH COMPLACENCY

In defence of Evangelicals in the USA, it is also important for British and other non-American Evangelicals to realize that however mistaken they might be, *at least they are trying to be salt and light in society.* For as the great British, Christian, nineteenth-century statesman Lord Shaftesbury once put it, the God who made men's souls made their bodies also. How active are British and other European Christians in trying to be effective witnesses to their own nations?

Perhaps part of the British problem is that when Christians did briefly run the country in the seventeenth century, during Cromwell's Commonwealth, it ended, from a spiritual point of view, in complete failure, and in a far shorter time than the American equivalent in New England. The Restoration period was one of the most decadent in British history, and it was not until the end of the eighteenth century that the United Kingdom saw the kind of Christian revival at grass roots level for which Cromwell and the Puritans often longed. For a while in the century or so after the Methodist Revival, British Christians of all denominations, such as Shaftesbury, William Wilberforce, Elizabeth Fry and others showed what a vast influence Christians could have out of all proportion to their numbers in society. However, by the twentieth century, similar people seem to have been very thin on the ground, and none have had the major impact of their nineteenth-century spiritual forebears.

As the parable of the mote and the beam reminds us, it is very easy to condemn others and be ignorant of your own faults. Whatever its faults, the American Church is one of the liveliest and most spiritually zealous on the earth. No Church can be perfect!

As I wrote this, an article appeared in the *Washington Post*, a journal that is often regarded with grave suspicion by many Evangelicals, most of whom read its local rival instead. But its author wrote to praise Evangelicals, not to attack them. In many strife-torn and dangerous parts of the world, he noticed, it was the Christian aid agencies that stayed behind with the poor and suffering, while the secular organizations had fled. Whatever he might think of Evangelicals politically, they were certainly living lifestyles consistent with their message of loving their neighbour as themselves. Or, as Christians would put it, they were living as salt and light in the world just as Jesus intended.

THE DANGERS OF MAKING ABSOLUTES OUT OF
WHAT ARE ONLY POLITICAL VIEWS

It is surely biblical behaviour like that which spreads the gospel effectively worldwide, rather than aggressive involvement by the Church as such in partisan politics. It is hard for the world to argue with Christians who are living like their Saviour, but very easy for them to ignore them when they are fighting politically on the world's own terms.

This is not to say that Christians ought to avoid the area of politics – very far from it! Both Wilberforce and Shaftesbury were active party politicians. They achieved the peaceful abolition of slavery and that of child labour respectively through the political process. But those towering achievements of theirs *as Christians* were to achieve such a consensus that good people of all political persuasions were to see and agree with the force of their arguments. Had all Christians been in only one political party, and had Christians been firmly identified with only one partisan point of view, it is very difficult to see how it could have happened as it did.

It is also perhaps worth pointing out that when Christians have been successful in the United Kingdom, it is because they have worked hard to show the logic of their beliefs to everyone. In the 1980s, Christian action was able, alas temporarily in the long run, to delay the turning of Sunday into a normal day of the week. They worked actively with Trade Unions on the political left and with pro-family Conservative Members of Parliament on the right, to defeat the Thatcher Government's ideologically driven programme to make Sunday into a regular working day.

In the light of the American equation between true godliness and Republican Party support, it is ironic that there are those in Britain who want to set up a Christian Democrat Party. Their politics are best summed up as Centre Left, in so far as they could be placed anywhere on the left/right spectrum. They are as convinced of the spiritual correctness of their policies as are those of the Christian Right in the United States.

The fact that two equally sincere groups of Christians have

come up with such totally different sets of policies is, to me, indicative of the problems into which Christians run when they seek to make absolutes out of what are man-made political opinions. There must surely be a profound difference between the saving work of Christ upon the cross, and the rate at which one should set income tax. To try to make the two equal is, in my view, to denigrate the Christian message of salvation.

Yes, we need far more Christians involved in the political process. But those Christians who are can always remember, as is thankfully the case with the many Evangelical members of the House of Commons, that their faith is at a far higher and eternal level of truth than their deeply held political convictions.

IF YOU DID HAVE A CHRISTIAN STATE, WHAT WOULD IT BE LIKE?

Historians of nineteenth-century America show that the denominational make-up of the infant state changed drastically. Whereas at independence most Americans were Congregationalist or Anglican, by the 1850s these two groups had shrunk to a far smaller proportion of the population. By far the biggest groups were those that had hardly existed in the 1770s, namely the Methodists and the Baptists.

In 1999 the figures were even more dramatic: there were, roughly speaking, over 30 million Baptists of different kinds, more than 13 *million* Methodists, but not much more than 60 *thousand* Congregationalists. Furthermore, today there are millions of Pentecostals, a denomination that did not even exist until the twentieth century.

Today Evangelical Christianity is very strong in these two more modern groupings, Baptists and Methodists. When America *did* have formal establishment, in Congregationalist Massachusetts and Anglican Virginia, Methodists were unknown and Baptists were persecuted.

So if we did have a Christian America, how would it be constructed? As we have just seen, the Founding Fathers wisely decided not to grant privileges to any one theological group because of the disadvantageous position into which that would put others. If Christianity were to have a formal role in the constitution of present-day America, what version of it would be chosen?

If it were to be a Protestant America, how would the 61 million Catholics feel about it, let alone the Jews, Hindus, Muslims and those of other faiths or none at all? What version of Protestantism would be chosen? How would Methodists and Pentecostals feel if the Baptists were to be the predominant denomination (and even in that instance, how would one choose between the different Baptist denominations)?

Even more problematic would be the spiritual question: how could you be sure that whatever version of Christianity was chosen would remain true to the gospel as understood by today's Evangelicals? For surely the history not just of New England but of denominations throughout the centuries has been that the faith of one generation is often more lukewarm in the next and hardly there at all in the third.

How many Methodists today could say that they believed exactly as Whitefield and the Wesley brothers once did? One of the reasons why there are so many denominations is that in every generation there are those who feel that the one they are in already has lost the way, and that it is necessary to start again. Would that not happen to any version of Christianity that was given a special *official* place in American society?

The early Church did not rely on state power to spread the message – it did the job itself. God's Church consists of God's people wherever they are, across the globe. The twenty-first-century Chinese Church is being heavily persecuted, and it is also growing.

HOW POWERFUL IS OUR GOD?

In conclusion, then, what I think we really need to ask is: *How powerful is our God?* Do we really believe that the low level of church attendance in the United Kingdom would go down further were the Church of England to be disestablished? Would the American churches become even more vibrant if there were prayer in schools (especially if it were to be on the same lines as those in England)? Is it God in whom we trust, or secular man-made laws? What makes a nation moral – is it legislation or people turning to faith in God?

We can see this in the types of law that gain national consensus and those that, however well meant, do not. The overwhelming mass of people normally – unless in unusual circumstances such as Nazi Germany – regard murder as wrong. There is thus a strong societal view that it is correct to have a law against murder, and this is the case even in societies that have become profoundly secular in outlook.

However, were a government to introduce legislation to make adultery illegal, as the Pilgrim Fathers tried to do centuries ago, it would now be impossible to enforce. It would be the same as the era of Prohibition in the USA, a cause supported strongly by Christians at the time. One can indeed argue that society is much more stable with secure and stable marriage as its basis. Many in the current British government are in fact saying just this, and significantly the defenders of marriage include secular as well as overtly Christian members of the Cabinet. Yet while the family as an institution is strongly supported by the government, and while divorce unquestionably breaks up that stability, they are not proposing to introduce legislation to outlaw divorce or to make adultery illegal. However strong the pragmatic, let alone Christian, reasons there would be in support of such a move, there would never be the societal consent for such legislation to be passed. As Jesus himself reminds us, divorce is against the will of God, but God permitted it in the Old Testament out of the hardness of people's hearts (Matthew 19.8).

It is possible – and here I am moving on to far more dangerous ground – that this is also the case with legislation on abortion. While the Christian case for describing it as murder is very strong, and while many on the political left would defend the foetus on the grounds of defending the weak and underprivileged, most people do not see abortion as murder. There is a case for saying that to make it illegal would not stop it but merely drive it underground, as was the case before the 1960s. This is not something that Christians can accept easily, and with good moral cause. But equally we do not try to force people by legislation to go to church (though such attempts were made both in sixteenth- and seventeenth-century England and in Puritan New England). And could one ever have a law that made covetousness illegal?

We live in a fallen world, and sometimes, like Christians of earlier ages, we forget what that means. Surely Francis Schaeffer was right in terms of a *scriptural* understanding of society when he said that what we need to do is to change the *mindset* that makes such things possible.

Here we can take heart. Jews, the mentally disabled and similar groups are no longer exterminated in Germany today, as they were in that very same country during the Nazi period. Italians in the twenty-first century do not take their pleasure seeing innocent people being killed and eaten by wild animals, as was the case with their Roman ancestors. There is no reason why God cannot work among Western men and women in our own time so that the slaughter of the unborn becomes equally unthinkable. The problem is not who is elected to the White House or who is appointed to the Supreme Court. The *real* problem is that for present-day Christians, our God is too small.

Conclusion

What this book has been arguing is that Christians are easily seduced by the spirit of their age. This is true especially in subtle ways that can be hard to spot. Perhaps the most seductive ideology of the past few centuries has been that of the nation, and here Christians have frequently been guilty of embracing its charms. In particular, we have forgotten the wise words of the psalmist: do not put your trust in princes.

This is, to me, what one could describe as a gospel issue, because it goes to the heart of what makes anyone a Christian. It was, as we saw, at the core of the Reformation: being born in Saxony, Geneva or Scotland did not in itself make you into a Christian – you had to be *born again*. But just like the generation of the Reformers, for whom this revolutionary return to New Testament doctrine still did not enable them to see the political ramifications of their rediscovery, we too have often been blind in terms of what it means for the relationship between Christians and the state in which they live.

There is one issue that I ought to deal with here first, to avoid misunderstanding, before reaching the final conclusion. Christians are people with an individual relationship with God, but all too often they want to transfer that direct relationship into one between God and the particular state in which they live – 'we live in a Christian country'. I have argued that that is biblically impossible. But there is always a danger that we go to the opposite end and adopt a hermit-like attitude to the secular world around us. This too is a mistake and, since we are commanded to be good citizens, we ought here to look at another aspect of the relationship between a Christian and the state. Otherwise we will fall from one extreme into the other, and be equally lacking in the balance of Scripture.

A TEMPTATION FOR THOSE WHO TAKE
CHRIST'S LORDSHIP SERIOUSLY

There is an especial temptation for Christians who have realized that Christ is our Lord as well as our Saviour. We see the fallen world around us, and long to do something. We understand from Scripture that we must be more than simply nice to our next-door neighbour, important though that is. We are salt and light in society generally. As both the apostles Paul and Peter remind us, God created governments for the well-being of humanity and if, as is the case in Britain and the United States, we live in a democracy, that gives us special opportunities to try to change things for the better.

However, when we do get involved in the wider world, we are in danger of forgetting why it is as it is – the fact of sin, of humanity's fallen nature. One of the tragedies of recent years is that Christians have all too often created a false separation between the two things Christ came to accomplish. Some are active in evangelism, proclaiming Christ as Saviour, while neglecting social involvement as they feel that it cannot be the true priority. On the other hand there are those whose activism in the wider arena – of which Christ is Lord – becomes so engrossing that they forget that the people among whom they are working are in desperate need of spiritual salvation. Surely this either/or approach is unhealthy and unscriptural? We ought to be involved in both, because if we truly love God and love our neighbours as ourselves, we should want them to come to salvation *and* live in better circumstances, the two things being compatible and not mutually exclusive.

I say all this because I would not want people to come away from reading this book with the idea that I am against active Christian involvement in our nation's affairs: far from it in fact. I have myself done advisory work for the British government, and have many good practising Christian friends in the world of politics, on both sides of the left/right political divide. In a democracy, there is a lot that members of the church can do, and have done over the centuries, to make the world a better place.

Let us take one issue in the news as I write this chapter – the environment and sustainable development. Christians believe that this planet is created by God, who commands us to exercise responsible stewardship over it. How much better it is if we get actively involved in matters such as responsible agriculture and use of resources, as against those who want selfishly to exploit our planet, or those who look at it in an almost pantheistic way and all but worship it.

WHAT IS IT THAT REALLY CHANGES THE WORLD?

Here we need to enter a note of caution, especially towards those deeply sincere Christians who feel that the affairs of their country can be made directly and politically subordinate to God. It is important to say that the motives of such people are impeccable, whatever abuse is hurled at them by aggressive secularists, who would deny religion any place in the public arena. But while I know that my fellow Christians mean well, I would say that their theology is sadly askew.

The early Church did not grow through state power but through that of the Holy Spirit, as the first Christians proclaimed the message of salvation. On the one hand it is true that God has in his sovereignty clearly worked through political circumstances – one only has to read the history of the Reformation to see that sympathetic princes or city councils made a huge difference. But on the other, it was, I would argue, the power of God that has enabled the Church to grow, and not the actions of any human political authority. Obviously, no Christian wants to be persecuted! It is much easier to practise one's faith in Britain or the United States than it is in China or Indonesia. But it is also significant that the Church is growing faster in countries where the government is remarkably unsympathetic than in states such as Britain or some of the Scandinavian states where an official Church–state link still exists.

WHAT EXACTLY DOES THE GOSPEL SAY?

We can see this if we consider Scripture. The first Epistle of Peter is perhaps the best place to do this. In writing to his recipients in what is now Turkey, he does so against a background of continuous persecution, which he describes as 'various trials' and fiery ordeals. Yet the Christians are to 'maintain good conduct among the Gentiles'. Even more extraordinarily, since it is the Roman authorities who are persecuting the Church, they are to be subject to the imperial authorities and to 'honour the Emperor'. Christian witness in such an environment, holiness and active evangelism are seen throughout the Epistle not as separate entities but as part and parcel of the Christian life.

From the point of view of the main theme of our book, perhaps the most important thing he writes is his description of who the Christians are as a people, and what their identity is generically.

> But you are a chosen race, a royal priesthood, a holy nation, God's own people, that you may declare the wonderful deeds of him who called you out of darkness into his marvellous light. Once you were no people but now you are God's people; once you had not received mercy but now you have received mercy.
>
> Beloved, I beseech you as aliens and exiles to abstain from the passions of the flesh that wage war against your soul. (1 Peter 2.9–11 RSV)

During the Reformation, this was often used as a key text in the resurrection of the biblical concept of the 'priesthood of all believers'. As we saw earlier, one of the most radical concepts of that time was the rediscovery of the teaching that ordinary Christian people did not need a special priesthood to mediate between them and God, or to interpret the word of God for them. This interpretation is surely correct, and it has been a source of considerable liberation for ordinary Christians ever since.

BACK TO PRIMARY SELF-IDENTITY

But I think that one can legitimately argue that it is more than this. Here we come full circle to the issue of identity that we saw in the first chapter. What is our *prime* self-identity and source of allegiance as Christians? Clearly in terms of legitimate demands the state has a call upon our loyalty because we are enjoined to obey the authorities and to honour them – even, as in Peter's time, those rulers who were actively persecuting the church. But Peter had discovered that his *primary* loyalty was now entirely different: a converted Roman centurion, the embodiment of the political oppressors of his ethnic nation, the Jews, was now his brother in Christ.

As Luke's frank narrative shows, Peter found this a very difficult conclusion to reach. This is entirely understandable. I am glad to be British and enjoy being so, and I have enormous affection for my wife's country, the USA, where I have the pleasure of spending much of my working life. If we live in such agreeable countries, we are very privileged; and there are millions of people in other nations who, while hating the regime in power, still enjoy being citizens of their particular state in many other respects.

But in showing us very explicitly who we are as Christians, Peter is telling us that we as Christians are, in a most profound way, 'aliens and exiles' here on earth – which is why I quoted from verse 11 as well as just from verses 9 and 10. We should never forget that as Christians we are a 'holy nation ... God's own people'. The country into which we are born can ask many things of us, from paying taxes to upholding the law. As Christians commanded by God to love our neighbours, we cannot be indifferent to what happens around us, and to the state of the society in which we live. But biblically, if we are to understand Peter properly, we cannot make our primary source of identity something that is only political or geographic, such as a state or ethnic group. The Church is the bride of Christ, and will be with him in eternity, long after this present world has vanished.

We should be Christians first and last. A nation that has in it many people who reject the gospel message cannot, by definition, be called a 'holy nation', nor can it ever be described as 'God's own people', because only the Church can by its very nature be so named. We will never get a perfect world this side of Christ's return.

As even a cursory glance at Old Testament books such as Kings or Chronicles shows us very vividly, the Children of Israel had God's law, but there were many kings and subjects who disobeyed God and defied his law. It is only through the new birth, through salvation in Christ, through *inward* change, that any society can be transformed, and even so we will continue to be sinners as long as we live. That is why a Christian country cannot exist. God's people are in every nation, race, ethnic and linguistic group across the earth; it is *they* who are God's own people, whether the political state they live in is British, American, Nigerian, Chinese, Peruvian or whatever. It is not a question of whose side God is on, but whether we are on God's side.

Bibliography

Anderson, Benedict, *Imagined Communities: Reflections on the Origin and Spread of Nationalism*. London, Verso, 1991.

Cameron, Euan K., *The European Reformation*. Oxford, Clarendon Press, 1991.

Catherwood, Christopher, *A Crash Course on Church History*. London, Hodder & Stoughton, 1998.

Catherwood, Christopher, *Five Leading Reformers*. Fearn, Christian Focus, 2000.

Catherwood, Christopher, *Why the Nations Rage: Killing in the Name of God*. London, Hodder & Stoughton, 1997; 2nd edn, Lanham MD and Oxford, Rowan and Littlefield, 2002.

Catherwood, Fred, *Jobs, Justice, Homes & Hope*. London, Hodder & Stoughton, 1997.

Catherwood, Fred, *Pro-Europe?* Leicester, IVP, 1991.

Colley, Linda, *Britons: Forging the Nation 1707–1837*. New Haven, CT and London, Yale University Press, 1992.

Davies, Norman, *The Isles: a History*. London, Macmillan, 1999; Papermac, 2000.

Greenfeld, Liah, *Nationalism: Five Roads to Modernity*. Cambridge, MA and London, Harvard University Press, 1992.

Hastings, Adrian, *The Construction of Nationhood: Ethnicity, Religion and Nationalism*. Cambridge, Cambridge University Press, 1997.

Holloway, David, *A Nation Under God*. Eastbourne, Kingsway, 1987.

Hosking, Geoffrey, and Schöpflin, George, eds., *Myths and Nationhood*. London, Hurst, 1997.

Johnston, O. R., *Nationhood: Towards a Christian Perspective*. Oxford, Latimer House, 1980.

Noll, Mark, *American Evangelical Christianity: an Introduction*. Oxford, Blackwell, 2001.

Noll, Mark, ed., *Christianity in America: a Handbook*. Tring, Lion, 1983.

Noll, Mark, *A History of Christianity in the United States and Canada*. London, SPCK, 1992.

Noll, Mark, *The Scandal of the Evangelical Mind*. Leicester, IVP, 1994.

Paxman, Jeremy, *The English: a Portrait of a People*. London, Michael Joseph, 1998.

Schaeffer, Francis, *A Christian Manifesto*. Basingstoke, Pickering and Inglis, 1981.

Schaeffer, Francis, *Genesis in Space and Time*. London, Hodder and Stoughton, 1972.

Schama, Simon, *Landscape and Memory*. London, HarperCollins, 1995.

Smith, Anthony D., *Nations and Nationalism in a Global Era*. Cambridge, Polity Press, 1995.